The
EDITOR IN CHIEF

A Management Guide
for Magazine Editors

Second Edition

The
EDITOR IN CHIEF

A Management Guide
for Magazine Editors

Second Edition

BENTON RAIN PATTERSON

COLEMAN E.P. PATTERSON

Blackwell
Publishing

Benton Rain Patterson was formerly an associate editor of The Saturday Evening Post, an articles editor for The New York Times Magazine, editor of Dominion magazine and managing editor of Guideposts magazine. He is emeritus associate professor of journalism at the University of Florida in Gainesville and author of the book Write to Be Read.

Coleman E.P. Patterson is associate dean of the Kelley College of Business and associate professor of management at Hardin-Simmons University in Abilene, Texas.

© 1997 Benton Rain Patterson and Coleman E.P. Patterson
© 2003 Benton Rain Patterson and Coleman E.P. Patterson

Blackwell Publishing Professional
2121 State Avenue, Ames, Iowa 50014

Orders: 1-800-862-6657
Office: 1-515-292-0140
Fax: 1-515-292-3348
Web site: www.blackwellprofessional.com

Authorization to photocopy items for internal or personal use, or the internal or personal use of specific clients, is granted by Blackwell Publishing, provided that the base fee of $.10 per copy is paid directly to the Copyright Clearance Center, 222 Rosewood Drive, Danvers, MA 01923. For those organizations that have been granted a photocopy license by CCC, a separate system of payments has been arranged. The fee code for users of the Transactional Reporting Service is ISBN-13: 978-0-8138-1079-9; ISBN-10: 0-8138-1079-5/2003 $.10.

Printed on acid-free paper in the United States of America

First edition, 1997 Iowa State University Press
Second edition, 2003 Iowa State Press

Library of Congress Cataloging-in-Publication Data
Patterson, Benton Rain
    The editor in chief: a management guide for magazine editors / Benton Rain Patterson and Coleman E.P. Patterson.—2nd ed.
        p. cm.
Includes index.
ISBN 13: 978-0-8138-1079-9 (alk. paper)
    1. Journalism—Editing. 2. Journalism—Management. I. Patterson, Coleman E. P. II. Title.
    PN4778.P38 2003
    070.4′1—dc21   2002015936

The last digit is the print number: 9 8 7 6 5 4 3

Contents

Preface

This book is intended to provide help and insight to anyone who works in the editorial department of a magazine, or wants to, but it is primarily intended to help equip the person who may one day become or has recently become the editor, the person who is charged with managing the editorial product, the editorial process and the editorial department—that is, the editor in chief.

When the book was first published, the authors were thinking only of traditional, print magazines. Since then, however, a new phenomenon in magazine publishing has commanded attention, requiring treatment in a magazine-editing textbook. That phenomenon, of course, is online publishing, which offers not only a new medium for established magazines but a singular opportunity for magazine entrepreneurs, both professional and amateur. And so this second edition of our book includes a chapter that may open readers' eyes to new entrepreneurial possibilities in magazine publishing and that gives guidance for the launching of an online publication.

The book is the work of two authors, one a former magazine editor and former teacher of aspiring magazine editors, the other a management and entrepreneurial specialist and teacher of aspiring managers and entrepreneurs. The result of the collaboration, we both hope, is a book that provides practical help in the making of successful magazines and in the making of successful magazine-editing careers.

Benton Rain Patterson
Coleman E.P. Patterson

The
EDITOR IN CHIEF

A Management Guide

for Magazine Editors

Second Edition

CHAPTER 1

Magazines and How They Work

Long before there were printing presses, movable type or even many people who could read, there were magazines. They weren't something to read, however. Back then the word (derived from the old French *magazin*, the Italian *magazzino* and the Arabic *makhazin*) was used to mean "storehouse." A magazine then was a place where goods of all kinds were kept. The word still has that meaning in one of its current usages.

From a place that contains all sorts of good things—such as a discount store's warehouse—to a publication that contains all sorts of good things was an easy leap for the word. The connection between the two kinds of interesting collections is easy to make.

What Is a Magazine?

Although the word still has several meanings, to English speakers today a magazine is, first of all, a periodical containing a collection of articles, stories, features, photographs and other pictures.

Modern magazines generally are a hybrid, a cross between books and newspapers. From the book strain they get the characteristic of lengthier and more literate writing. From books they also get their binding. Newspapers are not bound; toss one into the air and its pages will separate and scatter. Throw a magazine into the air and it will return to earth in one piece; the pages are bound together, like the pages of a book.

Magazines also get from the book strain some of their language. Issues of a magazine, for example, are often called "books"; sometimes the magazines themselves are called "books"; what are called "headlines" in a newspaper are generally called "titles" in magazines; what are called "reporters" on a newspaper are called "writers" or "authors" on magazines; a typewritten article or printout that would be called "copy" on a newspaper is a "manuscript" on magazines; what is "the front page" or "page one" on a newspaper is "the cover" on magazines.

From the newspaper strain magazines get the characteristics of timeliness, journalistic reporting and writing (generally speaking), periodic publication, sales by subscription, newsstand distribution and the publication of advertising.

Magazines, however, are more than a blend of other media. Magazines generally are distinguished by their attention to visual appeal, not only with their illustrations but in the use of white space, typography and the artistic display of their contents. Magazines, since about the 1860s, have been characterized by their marriage of text and pictures. It's not only the articles and features that make a magazine, but illustrations and photographs that, together with the text, are the alluring, enjoyable objects that readers can find in the storehouse.

Kinds of Magazines

When they go looking for jobs on a magazine, aspiring editors are likely to discover there are not only more magazines than they had realized but more *kinds* of magazines than they had thought, particularly if their idea of a magazine is the kind they've seen on the sales racks in supermarkets and convenience stores.

The diversity of magazines is so great that it's difficult even to devise classifications for them. But let's try anyway.

Magazines can be divided first into three broad, all-inclusive categories: (1) *commercial* magazines, which include those magazines that are intended to make a profit for their owners, along with not-for-profit magazines that sell subscriptions and/or single copies of the magazine, and in many cases also sell advertising space; (2) *public relations* magazines, which are not intended to make money but instead are meant to convey their owners' messages to their audiences; and (3) *others*. Let's take those three groups one by one.

Commercial Magazines

These publications break down into two large groups, which together comprise the bulk of magazines published in America.

Consumer Magazines They are so called because they are aimed at consumers—consumers of food, clothing, VCRs, automobiles, shampoo, nail polish, lawn mowers, ballpoint pens, whatever. These magazines come in two varieties:

■ Magazines that are *sold* to their readers, either by subscription or single-copy sales, commonly called newsstand sales, or by both subscription and single-copy sales. These are the magazines that are found in the racks at supermarkets, convenience stores, drugstores, bookstores and wherever else magazines are sold. They are probably the ones that most people think of when they think of magazines.

■ Magazines that are distributed *free*, either through the mail or at certain kinds of locations, such as restaurants, travel agencies, car rental offices, hotels and motels. Some are distributed aboard airlines. A great many are devoted mainly to entertainment, dining and travel subjects.

Trade Magazines These are also called business magazines and are aimed at audiences made up of people who have the same profession or occupation or trade, or work in the same industry, or own or manage the same kind of business, or otherwise have in common the way they earn a living or make money. Some examples: *Advertising Age, Food Topics, Gift & Stationery Business, Travel Agent, Nursery Retailer.*

Trade magazines come in two varieties:

■ Those that have paid subscriptions and, in some cases, are also sold on newsstands. *Folio:*, for example, the trade magazine of the magazine publishing industry, has a paid circulation. That means that readers must pay for the magazine. *Editor & Publisher*, the trade magazine of the newspaper publishing industry, is sold by subscription and in some large cities can also be bought on certain newsstands.

■ Those that are distributed free, usually through the mail.

One of the unusual characteristics of a trade magazine is that not everyone can get it. Generally speaking, anyone who has the price of a consumer magazine, either the subscription price or the single-copy price, can buy it. Not so with trade magazines. Most trade magazines have a *controlled circulation*. Their publishers restrict the magazines' circulation to those persons who qualify as members of the magazine's intended audience.

For example, the publisher of a trade magazine going to plumbers wants only plumbers and other people connected with the plumbing trade to get the magazine. Why? Because the price of an ad usually depends on the magazine's circulation—that is, the number of people who receive the magazine, whether they pay a subscription fee or receive the magazine free. The more circulation the magazine has, the more the advertiser must pay for an ad in it. But the advertiser wants the people who get the magazine to be genuine prospects for the product or service he's advertising. If only half of the magazine's audience are plumbers, for example, only half are potential customers for the plumbing-equipment advertiser. Therefore the advertiser would be wasting half of the money that the ad cost him if he placed his ad in a magazine whose audience was 50 percent plumbers and 50 percent something else. Business men and women who want to stay in business don't waste money that way.

Knowing that, the magazine's publisher or advertising representative wants to be able to tell the advertiser that virtually every person in the magazine's audience is a potential customer for the advertiser's product or service. The magazine doesn't want non-plumbers as subscribers or recipients because the advertiser doesn't want them.

To qualify for a subscription to a controlled-circulation magazine, or to continue receiving it if it is distributed free, the subscriber or recipient ordinarily must provide certain information to the magazine, documenting that he or she has the characteristics the magazine requires.

Public Relations Magazines

Public relations magazines especially include house organs (sometimes called budgeted publications), which come in two varieties:

Internal House Organs   These are published by corporations, institutions and organizations to communicate with employees, members, alumni or other constituents.

External House Organs   These are published by corporations, institutions and organizations to communicate with customers or clients, prospective customers or clients, suppliers, legislators, members of regulatory agencies, shareholders, potential shareholders, opinion-makers and VIPs of varied descriptions, according to the public relations aims and the nature of the company, institution or organization that publishes the magazine.

Other Magazines

The following five categories are a sampling of the many kinds of magazines available:

Literary Magazines   These are also called little magazines. They generally have a small circulation and little advertising, are heavy on text and light on illustration. Some examples: *Antioch Review, Carolina Quarterly, The Paris Review.*

Sunday Magazines   These are supplements to newspapers. Some examples: *Sunday Magazine,* supplement to the Sunday edition of Denver's *Rocky Mountain News; Tropic Magazine,* supplement to the Sunday edition of *The Miami Herald; The New York Times Magazine.*

Professional and Academic Journals   These are periodicals that publish reports on research in a particular professional, scientific or academic field and, in some cases, articles on the practice of the profession. Some examples: *American Journal of Cosmetic Surgery, Nutrition in Clinical Practice, New England Journal of Medicine.*

Single-Advertiser Magazines   These are magazines sponsored by one advertiser, with ads for the advertiser's products or services throughout the magazine. Such magazines generally run content that helps promote the use of the advertiser's products or services.

One-Shot Magazines   These are not periodicals, but they are magazines in every other respect. They are magazines that publish only one issue, and that issue is built around a single theme or subject. Each piece of content relates to that theme or subject. One-shots are usually sold only on newsstands.

Economics of Magazine Publishing

Except for public relations magazines, the continued existence of which ordinarily does not depend on their ability to produce revenue of their own, magazines generally are expected to make money. If they are not profitable or do not eventually become profitable to their owners, they usually cease to exist. Publishing a magazine is, after all, a business, and businesses that don't make money go out of business.

Magazines make money from two main sources:

1. Advertising. For most magazines the sale of advertising space is the major source of revenue. The rates they charge the advertisers are based on circulation and the quality of the audience. For example, a page of advertising in a leisure magazine for physicians is likely to cost an advertiser a lot more than a page ad in a magazine for stamp collectors.

Advertising rates are usually measured by their cost per thousand, or CPM ("M" being the abbreviation for mille, or thousand). To compute the CPM, divide the price of a full-page ad by the thousands of circulation. So if a magazine with a circulation of 80,000 charges $2,400 for a page ad, the CPM is $30.

It's the CPM and the characteristics of the audience that matter most to advertisers. The audience must be the people the advertiser wants to reach, and the CPM must be competitive with the CPM of other advertising media, especially other magazines.

Ads that come to the magazine from an advertising agency are billed to the ad agency, and when payment is made to the magazine, the amount is less than the price of the ad. That's because the ad agency gets a percentage, ordinarily 15 percent, of the price of the ad as its fee for developing the ad and placing it for the advertiser. So if the price of an ad placed by an agency is $2,400, the magazine will receive $2,040 from the agency, and the agency will bill the advertiser for $2,400, making $360 on the ad. A magazine can expect national and regional advertisers to use advertising agencies.

2. Circulation. Subscriptions provide a significant amount of revenue for many magazines, and others receive a substantial part of their total revenue from single-copy sales.

In the case of single-copy sales, the magazine makes an arrangement with a distributor—a national distributor if the magazine has a nationwide circulation, or with one or more regional distributors if the magazine has only a regional circulation. Distributors charge the magazine a percentage of the cover price to place the magazine on newsstands. The magazine usually gets half of the cover price, and the other half is split between the national distributor, the regional distributors (or wholesalers) and the dealers (the store owners, or retailers). So if the price on the cover of the magazine is $3, the magazine gets $1.50 for each copy sold, and the rest goes to the distributors and retailer.

Newsstand copies of the magazine are sold on consignment. Copies not sold are usually picked up by the wholesaler after several days or a couple of weeks and discarded. The distributor provides the magazine's publisher with a report on the number of copies sold and the number unsold and destroyed.

In the case of subscriptions, ordinarily the price of the first year's subscription is offset by the cost of acquiring the subscription, and magazines usually do not make money from subscribers until they renew their subscriptions. However, only the most successful magazines manage to get more than about half of their first-year subscribers to renew. That means that when a magazine gets new subscribers, it will probably lose about half of them when their subscriptions expire. The half that the magazine loses must then be replaced by additional new subscribers.

A much higher proportion of those who renew the first time ordinarily renews again in following years. For example, if 55 percent of new subscribers renew at the end of their first year's subscription, 75 percent of those who renewed may renew again at the end of their second year's subscription. And of the 75 percent who renew for a third year an even greater proportion, say 85 percent or more, are likely to renew when their third-year subscription is about to expire. (Those percentages are merely to illustrate the phenomenon; real-life percentages are not so predictable.)

Magazines that have high rates of renewal rates usually are successful, because they receive a significant amount of revenue from subscriptions *and* because high renewal rates indicate reader loyalty, which is often persuasive to advertisers who are being asked to place their ads in those magazines. For some magazines, such as *Consumer Reports*, circulation is the major source of revenue, since they do not run advertising.

Many magazines exploit other ways to generate revenue from their readers. It's a common practice for magazines to rent their subscription lists to other magazines and to other businesses that sell products through direct-mail solicitation. List rental can generate a substantial amount of revenue for magazines that have an audience with desirable demographic characteristics, such as heaps of disposable income.

Some magazines use their lists to sell their own merchandise, such as books, tapes, records and compact disks. Other magazines use house ads (their own ads in the magazine) to sell such things as books, calendars, house plans, dress patterns, recipes, toy models, T-shirts and caps bearing the magazine's logo, as well as a host of other items.

Some magazines also make extra money through subsidiary use of their content, allowing other magazines or book publishers to republish their photographs and articles.

Fundamentals of Starting a Magazine

Hundreds of new magazines are started every year, and not all of them by large corporations with vast resources. Many are started by individuals—editors or publishers or merely people with special knowledge about some area of human activity—who are working without the resources of a large organization. Regardless of whether the launch—that is, the starting, or start-up, of a new magazine—is by a thriving magazine-publishing company or by a hopeful entrepreneur, the successful start of a new magazine requires several basic steps:

1. Identify an audience. The days of mass circulation, general interest magazines are long gone. Magazines now need a niche, a place in the population mass where they can fit. They need to find a sizable group of people who share an interest or a demographic characteristic. They need a specialized audience (rather than a general audience)—an audience that is made up of, say, women over 50 or windsurfers or baseball-card collectors or managers of hazardous-waste disposal companies or cosmetology-school operators.

2. Identify advertisers. Who, the magazine entrepreneur must ask, wants to speak to that audience? What kinds of advertisers, and which advertisers in particular, are likely to be interested in reaching that audience with their advertising messages? For most magazines, advertising is the key to success, and a new magazine must have a clear and accurate idea of who its prospective advertisers are.

3. Conceive an editorial product to deliver editorial and advertising messages to its readers. It's not a brochure or a flyer; it's a magazine that is intended to carry the advertisers' messages. And so the entrepreneur must come up with a magazine that the members of the specialized audience will find interesting or useful or both, especially if copies of the magazine are to be sold rather than given away. If the editorial product—that is, the magazine that is the vehicle for the advertisers' messages—is not interesting to the intended audience, the audience members won't buy it or read it and won't see or respond to the advertisers' messages, which they must do if the magazine is to succeed.

4. Create a distribution plan. There has to be a way to get the magazine into the hands of the readers, and the magazine's planner must decide how. Will it be sold by subscription and distributed through the mail? Will it be distributed on newsstands? Will it be sent free to a list of people who constitute the magazine's intended audience? Will it be given away at supermarkets, or brokers' offices, or bicycle stores? A plan to distribute the magazine is needed.

5. Draw up a business plan. Anyone starting a magazine, or any other sort of business for that matter, should have a plan. He or she should anticipate the things that must be done, when they are to be done, how much money will be needed to do them, where the money will come from and when it will be available. A good business plan for magazines will have two parts: (1) a list of basic assumptions, including estimates of circulation, subscription price, newsstand price, number of ad pages, ad rates and so on; and (2) a set of cash projections, showing where and when the expense money is going and where the revenue money is coming from and when it is coming. (For detailed help on the preparation of a business plan, prospective entrepreneurs should see Leonard Mogel's book *The Magazine.*)

6. Raise money. It's going to take capital, enough to launch the magazine and carry it to the point where it makes more money than it spends—a point where cash from revenue flows in in time for it to flow out for expenses. This is the really hard part of starting a magazine. It's what separates the doers from the dreamers. Would-be publishers who don't have money of their own to finance the magazine must raise money from relatives or friends or people or companies that are likely to be interested in the proposed magazine.

It's usually a good idea for entrepreneurs in search of money to take with them their business plan and a dummy issue of the proposed magazine. The dummy issue will include a mock-up cover and inside pages, with ads, to give prospective investors or lenders a clear vision of what it is they're being asked to finance.

Raising venture capital—the money to start a new enterprise—is a specialized subject unto itself and far beyond the scope of this book. For those who are interested, however, the public library is a good place to start to learn how to go about trying to raise money to capitalize proposed magazines.

7. *Do it*. Once the money's been raised, the entrepreneuring editor or publisher goes on to the enjoyable parts of magazine publishing—creating and producing the issues.

Acquisition of Circulation

Magazines need readers, and there are just a few ways to get them.

One way is to distribute the magazine free in bulk. For example, a stack of magazines is left at cashier counters in restaurants, and the restaurant's customers pick up free copies when they stop at or pass the counter.

A second way is to distribute the magazine free to individual recipients, usually through the mail. What is needed is a list of people who have the shared interest or the demographic characteristics required for the magazine's audience. The magazine must use either an existing list or lists, or must compile its own list, which can be a difficult task indeed.

A third way is to sell the magazine on newsstands, as explained above.

A fourth way is to sell subscriptions to the magazine, which is probably the most common way to acquire circulation, particularly for consumer magazines. Publishers often use a variety of methods to sell subscriptions. Here are the most widely used:

Publisher's Direct Mail   This method is familiar to anyone who has ever opened a mailbox. To the sender it's direct mail; to the recipient it's junk mail. Magazines that use direct mail to sell subscriptions— and virtually all do—go through an elaborate process to solicit subscriptions.

The first step in the process is to create a mailing piece, or have a direct-mail consultant create it. It's really more of a package than a piece, usually containing at least four components: (1) an outgoing envelope, usually a window envelope; (2) a letter that describes the magazine and presents the "sell" to the recipient; (3) an order card, usually with a label bearing the recipient's name and address affixed to the card; and (4) a business reply envelope, called a BRE, into which the order card and a check may be inserted and mailed to the magazine or the magazine's fulfillment agency. The fulfillment agency is a firm that maintains the magazine's subscription list and prints it out for the magazine whenever needed.

In some cases, usually depending on the nature of the magazine, the mailing piece will also include a four-color brochure, giving the recipient a lusher look at the product being offered and enhancing the sell. In other cases the mailing piece may combine the letter with the order card and perhaps not include a BRE. In that case the order card is a self-mailer. On one side of it is the order form, and on the other side are the name and address of the magazine or the magazine's fulfillment agency. Self-mailers might also be used in mailing pieces that contain a BRE, making the BRE nonessential but allowing new subscribers to include a payment check if they want to.

The next step in direct mail is to find some appropriate mailing lists—names and addresses of people who could be interested in the magazine and who might buy a subscription to it. The best way to find appropriate lists is to go (by telephone or fax) to a list broker, a firm that represents owners of lists, including other magazines, and brings list users and list owners together. The broker provides descriptions of the lists available, including the price for renting them (which is usually stated in an amount per 1,000 names), and can help the magazine identify the most appropriate, most promising lists.

The magazine then picks a few of the lists to test, which is the next step. Testing is the secret to success in direct mail. There are three elements that the magazine will test:

■ *The mailing piece.* Canny publishers will prepare not one mailing piece but two or more, each with a different approach to the recipient. Then they will test each one, to see which is most effective. Inclusion of a four-color brochure, for example, may make the mailing piece cost considerably more, but its inclusion may result in substantially more subscriptions being sold and therefore make the additional expense worthwhile.

■ *The offer.* A subscription to the magazine will be offered to the mailing piece's recipients at different prices. It may be offered with and without a premium, with and without free trial issues, with a special introductory price for six issues and with a special introductory price for 12, or 18, issues.

The magazine is looking for the offer that draws the best response and makes the most sense for the magazine. For example, a 12-month subscription that sells for $48 may draw fewer subscription orders than a 12-month subscription that sells for $36, but the additional $12 per subscription may offset the poorer response and mean more money to the magazine.

■ *The list.* The way to test a list is to sample it. The magazine will ask the list broker to pull, say, 2,000 names at random from each list to be tested. Only the lists that yield what the magazine considers a good response in the test mailing will later be used in the big mailing, often called a "roll-out."

Usually a magazine looks for a direct-mail response of around 3 percent, give or take a few tenths of a percentage point, or better. If a list—or a mailing piece or an offer—draws substantially less than, say, 2.7 percent, the publisher is likely to consider the response so poor that that list, or mailing piece or offer, is discarded. If a list, or mailing piece or offer, draws a response of 2.7 percent or better, then it is likely to be included in the big, main mailing.

Some magazines do their own mailings. They send out the mailing pieces and receive the order cards when they are returned by the new subscribers. Most magazines, however, prefer to have someone else handle those chores, which require special equipment, trained workers and, usually, a lot of building space. And so to complete the steps in the direct-mail process, they turn the work over to companies that specialize in such tasks.

Publishers choose a mailing house to: (1) receive the mailing piece components from the printer; (2) receive the lists from the list broker; (3) affix the lists' mailing labels to the order cards; (4) insert the order cards and the other components into the outgoing window envelopes and seal the envelopes; (5) sort the pieces for mailing; and (6) put the pieces into the mail.

Publishers choose a fulfillment service to: (1) receive the orders from the new subscribers; (2) keep track of the lists from which the orders are coming (the order cards are coded for that purpose) and report that information to the publisher; (3) input all the required data for each order into their computer system; (4) bill the new subscribers; (5) act as cashier when payments are made; (6) provide the publisher with a complete accounting, along with a check or electronic bank deposit; (7) maintain the list, updating the information on each subscriber and making address changes as needed; and (8) print out the list whenever the publisher requests.

An entrepreneur seeking the services of a direct-mail consultant, list broker, mailing house or fulfillment service can find listings of them in *Magazine Industry Market Place*, or *MIMP*, the all-inclusive directory of the magazine publishing industry. A copy of *MIMP* is available from the publisher, R.R. Bowker Company, 1180 Avenue of the Americas, New York, New York 10036, or can be found at almost any public or university library.

Direct mail is always subject to the vagaries of weather, season and prevailing economic conditions and is far from being an exact science. Furthermore, small, test mailings have a way of achieving better results than big mailings to the same lists, using the same mailing piece and offer. Direct mail is also expensive, running into hundreds of dollars per thousand pieces mailed, and it is enormously wasteful. Even a remarkably good response of, say, 4 percent means that 96,000 out of every 100,000 pieces mailed will go into the trash.

Direct mail, however, with good testing techniques, can be somewhat predictable, reducing the guesswork and gamble, and can also be the most efficient and the quickest way to acquire circulation. Outgoing mailing pieces are usually mailed third class, or bulk rate, to save on postage costs, and third-class mail ordinarily takes a couple of weeks to reach its recipients. Within two to three weeks after the mailing piece reaches the recipient, the magazine or its fulfillment service has practically all the orders that will come from the mailing. No other means of acquiring circulation will yield so many subscriptions in so short a time.

Co-op Direct Mail   This is a way of spreading the cost of direct mail. Instead of creating an entire mailing piece, with four or five components, and putting it into the mail, the publisher using co-op direct mail joins with other direct-mail advertisers and puts his magazine's selling piece in an outgoing envelope with those of several others, sharing the costs with the other advertisers.

Piggyback Direct Mail   This is another way of cutting costs on direct mail. The magazine cuts a deal with, say, a department store, and the department store puts the magazine's little selling piece into the envelopes containing the store's bills to its customers.

Radio and TV Ads   This is ordinarily an expensive way to acquire circulation, measured by the cost per subscription. Some magazines use radio and TV ads mostly to support their direct-mail campaigns or to boost single-copy sales.

Space Ads   These are ads published in newspapers and other magazines. They provide a surprisingly cost efficient way to acquire subscriptions, measuring cost by the amount of money spent per subscription order. The orders, however, tend to arrive in drips and dribbles over a relatively long period of time.

House Ads and Inserts   One of the cheapest and most effective ways to acquire circulation is to sell subscriptions in the magazine itself, by using house ads, blow-in cards (order cards inserted loose between the magazine's pages) or bind-in cards (subscription order cards that are bound into the magazine between its pages).

Direct-Mail Agencies   Examples of such agencies are Publishers Clearing House and Ebsco. The cost of acquisition is low compared to the magazine's own direct mail, but the magazine receives only a small percentage of the subscription price, and renewal rates tend to be much lower than renewal rates from the magazine's own mailings.

School Plans   These are programs conducted by subscription-sales organizations, using young students—and their parents—to sell subscriptions to raise funds for the school or school organizations.

Other Ways   They include catalog sales (made by companies that specialize in selling subscriptions to libraries and institutions), inserts in newspapers, and telephone agencies (subscriptions are solicited by companies specializing in sales by phone). Another way, infrequently used, is the purchase of the subscription list of a magazine going out of business. Often the cost for such a list is little more than the assumption of the failing magazine's subscription liability—that is, the issues owed to the individual subscribers. The failing magazine's audience needs to be similar to the buying magazine's audience. Even so, the renewal rate is likely to be extremely low.

Paid Circulation vs. Free Distribution

There are several big advantages to having a paid circulation, particularly subscriptions. The most obvious advantage is the subscription revenue, but there are others. Subscriber magazines can rent their subscription lists—both their expired list (the list of former subscribers) and their active list (their current subscribers). Also, potential advertisers are more likely to be persuaded to buy an ad if they know the audience has asked for the magazine and paid for it.

But there are disadvantages, too. The cost of acquiring subscriptions can be forbiddingly huge and the risk absolutely terrifying, especially for a small or start-up magazine. Even newsstand sales can prove a costly misadventure for new magazines, which cannot expect to sell more than 25 to 50 percent of the copies placed on the racks. In fact, a 50 percent sale would be considered good by many magazines. Meanwhile, the magazine has to pay the printer for 100 percent of the copies.

Furthermore, national distributors usually require a certain minimum number of magazines to distribute, upwards of 100,000, which means a new magazine's publisher must print enough copies of the magazine to satisfy the distributor and probably will not learn how well or poorly the newsstand sales did until about three issues have been printed and distributed.

Free distribution avoids those risks and costs. The great advantage of free distribution is that the magazine does not have to be sold in order to reach the hands of the reader. The huge outlay of cash and the risk associated with acquiring subscribers are avoided. And, unlike magazines sold on newsstands, the free-distribution magazine needs print no more copies than those that will actually reach members of the magazine's audience, thereby effecting a considerable savings on printing and paper costs.

To acquire readers—or at least recipients of the magazine—the free-distribution magazine's publisher needs only borrow, buy or compile a list of persons (or firms or organizations or institutions) that possess the required characteristics. In many cases those names, if not lists, are available from directories in public libraries.

The obvious disadvantage of free distribution is the lost opportunity for circulation revenue. Also, advertisers usually want some way of knowing that the people who receive the magazine actually read it and see their ads. And so the magazine must devise a way to find out which recipients want and read it, and which ones don't. A questionnaire, either in an issue of the magazine, often in the form of a bind-in card, or mailed separately, is the device many free-distribution magazines use to certify readership for advertisers and for the organizations that audit magazine circulation in behalf of advertisers.

Minimizing the Risk

Occasionally a magazine publisher, or prospective publisher, will attempt to take some of the gamble out of starting a new magazine by using focus groups or surveys of potential buyers of the magazine to determine audience interest in the proposed publication. Sometimes those techniques can help a publisher or editor shape the editorial product or more clearly define the intended audience, but many experienced publishers believe that until a prospective subscriber or newsstand buyer is actually asked to write a check or lay out cash for the magazine, there is no meaningful measure of a potential buyer's interest in the magazine. Entrepreneurs need to be cautious in the use of such devices.

Organization of the Magazine Publishing Enterprise

The structure of magazine publishing companies is ordinarily simple and based on function, no matter the kind of magazine. The size of each unit of organization naturally depends on the size of the magazine—the bigger the magazine, the more elaborate each of its parts is. But the organization of the parts, representing the division of duties and responsibilities, ordinarily is unvarying, regardless of the magazine's size. A typical organization would comprise five departments, or areas of responsibility:

Editorial Department

The people here, of course, are the ones who create and produce the editorial product, the magazine itself. The editor (or whatever the magazine calls the chief editor) is in charge, with a staff working under his or her direction. The editor is accountable to the magazine's publisher. (See Chapter 3 for more on the organization of the editorial department.)

Advertising Department

The people here sell and manage the magazine's advertising. The person in charge is the advertising director, who is accountable to the publisher.

Circulation Department

Here are the people who are responsible for getting the magazine into the hands of readers, whether by single-copy sales, subscriptions, free distribution or whatever. The circulation director is in charge and he or she is accountable to the publisher.

Promotion Department

People here have the job of making the magazine known or better known to advertisers, advertising agencies, potential readers and the trade, profession, business, interest group or other constituency served by the magazine. In charge is the promotion director, who is accountable to the publisher. On a small magazine, promotion is likely to be handled by someone in either the advertising or circulation department, rather than by a separate department.

Business Department

This part of the organization might instead be called administration or the publisher's office. Here are the people who keep the books, pay the bills, bill the advertisers, make out the payroll, complete the forms, file the reports—the magazine's housekeeping chores. In charge is the publisher, who answers to the owner (if the publisher isn't the owner) or to a board of directors.

For many magazines, particularly small or new ones, the lines between the departments are blurred. Workers on such magazines are often called upon to perform all sorts of tasks not ordinarily a part of their jobs. On many small magazines, the publisher is also the owner, the editor and the advertising director.

However, the usual division of duties, no matter how complex or simple the magazine's organization, puts *the* editor in charge of the creative part of the enterprise while the publisher concerns him/herself with the money-making and money-spending parts and the overall supervision of the enterprise.

CHAPTER 2

The
New
World of
Online
Magazines

Practically since the beginning of written communication, people have been inscribing or writing down their ideas or information, making copies of what's been written and then distributing the copies to others. Through many centuries the processes and methods of disseminating published material—copies of the original—have changed very little, until recently.

Also until recently the cost of publishing has always been related to the number of copies produced, a quantity associated with the number of people expected to be reached by the published material. Getting a publication into the hands of its intended audience, through mail or some other form of distribution, has been—and for most publications still is— a costly and time-consuming process. Moreover, updating or changing information in any way required a whole new publication—which then had to be redistributed to its audience. Now all of that is changing.

Introduction to Electronic Magazines

In the final decade of the twentieth century the historic methods of the publishing process began a speedy evolution. The widespread availability and use of the Internet began removing barriers that for centuries had been raised by traditional forms of communication. Time and cost limitations fell away in the rapid advance of new technology. Using Internet tools, individuals now can communicate with others across the country and around the world almost instantaneously and at practically zero cost. Audio, video, graphics and text can be transmitted by computer through cable and satellite communications networks to practically anywhere on Earth. The advancements in communications technology that occurred in the late twentieth century and are continuing in the twenty-first century are so revolutionary that even as recently as fifty years ago they were unimaginable to ordinary people.

The revolution in communications technology has had huge effects on the magazine and print-information industries. Through a variety of electronic communications media, text that formerly had to be printed for dissemination can now be sent or displayed almost instantly to audiences around the world at minimal cost. With employment of the new electronic technology, the costs of traditional production and distribution of print publications have been replaced by costs incurred only by the production of a new kind of publication. Through the wide availability of sophisticated word-processing and editing software, as well as graphic-design and image-editing programs and website and editing and design software, much of the magic of creating attractive, professional-looking publications has been placed in the hands of ordinary people with basic computer skills, who have access to computers.

The combination of near-zero distribution cost and access to low-cost electronic publishing tools (website design, word-processing, e-mail, graphics programs) has created an environment where nearly anyone with an interest or cause can create and electronically publish information and other messages on the web. This new forum for communication has allowed many aspiring writers/editors/publishers to express their ideas and convey their information to the world. Many traditional publishers have recognized the advantages of electronic publishing and have likewise moved onto the "information super-highway."

The Internet and Changes in Communication

The fundamental change in communication methods brought about by the Internet is not a whole lot different from the change brought about approximately a century ago by the telephone. With the invention of the telephone, individuals could suddenly communicate across the world with each other in real time. The changes effected by that technology reached throughout society. Today many of the same kinds of changes are occurring because of advances in information and computer technology. Low-cost and readily available communication technology has not only allowed casual communication to occur between people in new ways (e-mail, chat and instant-messaging sessions, web-based video conferencing) but also has permitted business to be conducted across greater distances in different and more efficient ways. For example, at-home consumers can use the Internet to comparison-shop and pay for products online, buying from merchants around the world, seeing current prices and inventory and not having to wait for printed, mail-out catalogs that may not accurately present prices or inventory and that require phone or mail-in orders. As evidenced in today's personal and business world alike, the Internet has opened new doors to communication, information access and methods of conducting business.

The telephone system is analogous to the Internet in regard to the influence it has had on information access and the ability to communicate with others across great distances; it also provides an illustration of how the Internet works and what is required to get onto the net. For someone to have an operable phone—one that can make and receive calls—the instrument must be hooked to the telephone network and have a phone number. Phone numbers are codes designed to tell the communications equipment where a particular telephone is located. A person wishing to reach another person via the phone system needs little more than a telephone from which to place a call, as well as the phone number of the person with whom he or she wishes to communicate. The key to the use of telephone communication, however, is the system by which the phones on both ends of the communication are hooked together through a network of lines, switches, relays and communications machinery.

The Internet is simply a network of computers—all hooked together through a set of wires, switches, relays and communication machinery. To access information on the Internet, a person merely needs a computer that is hooked to the worldwide web, plus a "number" (that is, a web address) for the computer that contains the information of interest. Instead of talking to a person on the other end of an Internet call, the person making the call sees the contents of a computer directory or subdirectory. The contents are computer files that are viewable with Internet browser software.

Electronic Magazines

Small publishers struggling under the burden of production and distribution costs have been quick to see the money-saving opportunity presented by the Internet. And the web has attracted not only small publishers. Large-circulation, established magazines have devised electronic editions of their publications for display on the screens of personal computers. In all, three kinds of e-magazines have sprung to life with the development of the Internet. They are:

E-Zines

One area of publishing that has made a natural transition from the printed to the cyber world is so-called zine publications. A zine is typically an amateur, low-budget publication produced by a single writer/editor/publisher or by a small group of like-minded producers. Profit is not the primary motivation for most zine publishers. Rather, zines exist to express the editors' concern or enthusiasm about some particular subject. Because most zines are not-for-profit or generate very little revenue, minimizing production and distribution costs is of vital interest to their publishers.

The range of zine topics is almost limitless. Newsletters and other kinds of publications that distribute information about a single topic might all be classified as zines. Original content, written and/or edited by the zine editor, is what ordinarily distinguishes a zine.

The electronic counterparts to printed zines are e-zines. The topics around which they are built range from poetry to computers, from financial management to religion. Like printed zines, most e-zines exhibit a passion for their subjects. The explosion of Internet use has allowed anyone with any interest to publish information to those who share that interest.

The advantages of publishing information on the web have inspired the creation of new e-zines and encouraged existing zine publishers to move their publications to the Internet, virtually eliminating production and distribution costs. Using e-mail address lists, e-zine publishers instantly distribute their electronic publications to recipients around the world.

Web-Zines

While the use of e-mail as a distribution system is popular with many zine publishers, it doesn't work for those who have no address list to which to mail, or who desire more than e-mail can provide, or who have other good reasons for not using e-mail. For those publishers the aim is to bring readers to their website, where text and graphics are displayed to all comers. Those website publications are known as web-zines.

Web-zines have an advantage over e-zines in that they allow publishers to incorporate graphics and other computer-memory features (including still pictures, video and audio files and other graphic features such as charts and graphs) that would prove difficult and/or time-consuming for e-mail programs to read or display. Web-zines can also make use of forms, discussion lists, interactive features and online subscription services and payments. Online reader surveys (with real-time results), question-and-answer forums, "chat with expert" sessions, automated bulletin board and classified ad postings, searchable and retrievable past issues and special video and audio programs for subscribers can all exist in the web-zine world. In addition, potential advertisers and sponsors can easily make contact with the web-zine's sales personnel through e-mail links from the website.

Web-Edition Magazines

The ability of web-zines to incorporate such electronic features gives them advantages over traditional print magazines, which is the big reason many established magazines now have web counterparts. The web versions of traditional magazines have not replaced the print versions, but instead serve as a complement to them, while also taking advantage of the cost and time savings of Internet publication.

In addition to providing the potential to attract web surfers who are unfamiliar with the printed magazine and inducing them to become subscribers to it, web-edition magazines offer other benefits to both the magazine's publisher and readers. Like web-zines, the web editions can incorporate interactive elements, which the print versions cannot. Web editions may not have the space limitations of their print counterparts. Pictures and text that didn't make it into the printed version can be readily included in the web edition. Updates of printed articles and late-breaking news developments can be quickly added to the web edition at any time—at practically no cost—and be made almost instantly available to viewers worldwide.

To combine the advantages of e-mail distribution with web-zines or web editions, publishers may e-mail their subscribers summaries of the content with links in the e-mail back to the web-zine or web edition. That technique, while almost an e-zine in itself, provides a way to attract readers to the magazine's website.

Electronic Magazines as a Hobby or Business

Although money-making is not the driving force behind the publication of most e-zines and web-zines, there are costs associated with producing an electronic magazine that must be met. Web editing software programs can cost several hundred dollars; website packages from web hosting services can have monthly charges, and e-mail distribution lists and charges for submitting site information to web search engines and directories entail costs also. Additionally, printed promotional materials (such as business cards, brochures, flyers) and advertising expenses online and off-line will also require money from the enterprise. There also is an opportunity cost to producing an electronic magazine, since time spent creating, promoting and updating it is time that cannot be spent on activities that do make money.

The sense of fulfillment that comes from publishing an electronic magazine may bring an intrinsic feeling of reward to the publication's writer/editor/publisher. Indeed, the passion and dedication exhibited by many e-zine and web-zine publishers seem to indicate that many of their enterprises exist primarily for such rewards, as well as for the benefits they perceive to subscribers and even to society as a whole. However, expenses must be paid somehow. Electronic publishers, or prospective publishers, who require their publications to pay their own way can generate revenue in the following ways:

Sell advertising space. As with traditional print publications, electronic magazine publishers may find companies that will pay to have their ad messages placed before the electronic magazine's readers. An e-zine or web-zine whose readers constitute a narrow market might be limited by the number of potential advertisers, but at the same time may have the advantage of being one of the few media that are focused on those advertisers' market. To increase the value of advertising in electronic magazines, hyperlinks can be provided to an advertiser's website.

Find a sponsor. Individuals, corporations or other organizations that are sympathetic to the publication's concerns may be willing to support sections of the publication or even the entire enterprise.

Sell subscriptions. On web-based zines, password protected sections of the magazine can be blocked off from nonsubscribers. Web surfers and prospective subscribers may browse through the public sections of the zine, but must become subscribers to view the entire contents. Subscription payments can be sent to the publisher through the mail, or in the case of the more technologically sophisticated electronic publisher, payments may be made with a credit card through a secured payment area of the website. The use of credit cards for payment requires an advanced understanding of web design and entails more costly web hosting services. For a relatively small fee, third-party payment services, like those offered to users of popular web auction sites, can relieve the electronic publisher of the burden of payment collection. Third-party payment companies will process customer credit-card transactions through their websites and will send you a check for the amount of money they collect for you, or will direct-deposit the money into your bank account, minus a modest transaction fee.

Earn sales commissions. Directing web visitors to a partner company's website may earn you sales commissions. Many large web businesses sponsor affiliates programs whereby links to the company's website are provided to partners' sites and commissions are paid to partners on any sales that result from a shopping session originating through the link on the partner's site. Affiliates programs pay finder's fees, or referral fees, to websites that direct business to another website. Such fees might be a fixed percentage or a sliding scale of percentages that increase as the amount of the sale increases. Other programs pay a flat dollar amount for a particular type of transaction that results while the customer is linked from an affiliate's website.

Affiliates programs do come with their share of disadvantages. Just as print publications' readers may be put off by excessive advertising in the magazine, visitors to your website can feel put off by too much commercialization of your website, by too many hyperlinks to merchants (which are usually banner ads prominently displayed on your website). Well-informed web surfers know about affiliates programs and can recognize affiliates' banners and links. It's possible that they could come to believe they are being exploited and resent the treatment.

The hyperlink from your site to the affiliate's site ordinarily includes a code that identifies your site as the path the shopper took to reach an affiliate's site. If an online shopper reaches the affiliate through your site and later returns to the affiliate's site without going through your site, you will not receive a commission. By directing web surfers from your site to the affiliate's site you end up steering them away from your site. Thus, if you provide hyperlinks to other sites, you should make sure the hyperlink is set up to open a new window in the Internet browser for the affiliate's site so that your website is not closed out on the computer screen.

In any case, website owners need to weigh the advantages of affiliates programs against the disadvantages of commercializing their sites, possibly alienating visitors, and diverting web traffic away from their sites.

One of the very best ways to have the online publication pay for itself is to pay strict attention to the costs of running the enterprise. An entrepreneurial publisher can use a variety of techniques to ease the cash requirements of the publication. In business these techniques are known as "bootstrap financing" techniques—internal methods to reduce the costs of production and to create profits out of what is already owned. Here are some of those techniques:

■ Instead of purchasing web editing software, create your web page in your word-processing program. Colors, fonts, images and background textures can all be manipulated in word-processing programs and saved in html format. Microsoft Word will even let the user save the document directly to a remote site via an ftp option. Ftp (file transfer protocol) is the process by which computer files are copied between your personal computer's hard drive and the hard drive of the host server computer. Free ftp software can be downloaded from a variety of Internet software sites.

■ Instead of paying for Internet access, you can sign up for an account with a free Internet service provider (ISP). Doing so could save several hundred dollars a year. The price you pay for free Internet access is your having to put up with advertising banners on your screen while you are online. In many cases, it's a price worth paying.

■ Find a free host server instead of paying for web space. Internet service providers frequently give web space to service subscribers. Other sites may provide free web space, but the price you pay is the display of the service's advertising banners on your site.

■ Manually submit your website's information to web search engines and directories instead of paying a company to do it for you. Find out which search engines and directories are the most popular and manually do a "submit site" request to them to have your site included. Make sure you read the submission directions for the engine/directory to learn how to enter the keywords that will be the most effective in drawing searchers to your site.

■ Create your own e-mail distribution list. Search the Internet for sites related to yours and you might find some with discussion lists, a device whereby individuals submit questions and post information. By discovering several such sites and copying e-mail addresses of participants, you can create your own e-mail distribution list. Once you have captured those names and addresses, write and send a friendly e-mail to them, along with a request that the recipient visit your website or accept an introductory copy of your e-zine. That technique is a quick and easy—not to mention inexpensive—way to get the word out about your publication and create or increase your circulation base.

How to Get Started with Your Online Magazine

To create a website that allows Internet surfers to reach and read it, you will need three essentials:

Host server. The host server is a computer that is connected to the network of computers known as the Internet. The host server is where your web files are stored. These servers remain up continuously and ordinarily are able to handle high levels of Internet traffic. What the host server provides may be as simple as blank space on which to load your web pages, but may also be as elaborate as "packages" that include databases, encryption technology for secure online payments, and video and audio streaming abilities. Of course, the more services you wish from your host server, the more you will pay. As stated earlier, some companies will provide free web space in exchange for the display of the host's advertising banners on your website.

You can find hosting services on the web by using an Internet search engine or directory.

Web address. You must have a URL—a Uniform Resource Locator. It is your web address. If you use web space provided by a host at no cost, you will probably have little choice in selecting your web address. Such free services allow you to choose an account name that becomes part of the URL, or web address, for your site. For example, AT&T assigns web addresses in the following format: http://*youraccountname*.home.att.net. All subscribers to AT&T's Internet service packages receive such an address.

To customize a web address to the name of your enterprise, you need to reserve a web address through a domain-name registration service. To find such a service, enter "domain name registration" on the search line of an Internet search engine or directory. The most common customized web addresses have *.com* or *.org* or *.net* as extensions. New ones, such as *.biz*, *.info*, and *.name*, are also available. Be sure to comparison-shop several domain-name registration companies and check out their offerings and prices. Choosing a web address is very important; it needs to be one that people can easily remember and readily identify as your site.

Website content. The content is of course the soul and substance of your online magazine. Whether the content is original or picked up from other sources, it is the publication's reason for being. The presentation of content on your website can be as simple or as complex as desired. A page of text written in recently released word-processing programs can be saved as an html file and copied to the host server (via ftp) to become a simple, plain-vanilla page for your readers. Adding pictures and colors is the easiest way to enhance the pages' appearance. For a more professional-looking product, you can buy and use web editing software packages that can be manipulated like word-processing programs but provide more advanced editing and display techniques. Some host servers provide website templates, whereby the editor simply enters information into pre-designed formats that are automatically published to the web.

E-Zine Distribution

If your plan is to launch an e-zine using e-mail distribution, without a website, you will need some sort of e-mail service to set up and maintain your e-mail list. You can pay for one that is part of an Internet-service subscription or, in keeping with a shoestring budget, you can subscribe to a free e-mail service. Your e-mail distribution list can be managed and stored in your e-mail program's address book or it can be managed in a word-processing program that allows the list to be copied and pasted into the address line of the e-mail message.

E-Zine Graphics

E-mail zines in the past have been limited in their ability to display their content with attractive graphics, but by saving your e-zine pages as html files and attaching them to e-mail for distribution, the layouts, color and graphics of an html page can be sent to recipients. The drawback of this technique, of course, is that file sizes increase as more graphics are used, thereby increasing downloading time for your e-zine's subscribers and possibly requiring you to acquire additional memory to store back issues of the e-zine.

How to Promote Your Online Publication

Until the potential readers of your online publication actually see your product, your publishing venture will be no more than a private hobby. The big trick—the key to success—is getting your publication before the eyes of the people for whom it is intended. You will have to promote your publication if you want to maximize its potential.

Taking a venture into the cyber world creates promotional obstacles that print magazines do not ordinarily face. Unlike a print magazine, an online magazine isn't left lying on the coffee table of a host, or doesn't stand in a rack at the dentist's office or at the supermarket or the public library or any other such place where someone unfamiliar with the publication may be introduced to it and sample it. Online magazines do not benefit from pass-along, the phenomenon whereby print magazines move from one reader to another. To promote their products, online magazine publishers need to employ the usual means of promotion—such as getting listed in the telephone directory's yellow pages and in business directories and calling attention to the publication's address on business cards, brochures and other printed materials. They also need to learn ways to promote their publications in the cyber world. Here are some of those ways:

■ The cyber equivalent of getting a telephone number listed in the telephone directory and yellow pages is having your web-zine site listed with Internet search engines and directories. Many hosting services offer submission services, for which you pay to have them submit your site information to a number of search engines and directories (and which may be included in a grand directory of websites, organized by topic). With a little research and time, however, you can do your own submissions and save yourself some money.

Ordinarily, search engines automatically scan your site for keywords that will place your site in their search-results lists. Your inclusion of pertinent keywords in your site is therefore extremely important and must be given careful consideration.

■ A popular way to attract visitors to your web-zine is through the creation of a banner advertisement that is displayed on other websites. Exchanging banner ads with other websites can be done informally by contacting other website owners or can be done for you by companies offering such a service. To use such a service, you will have to display banners of other companies on your site; and in exchange, other sites will display your banners.

Banner display packages can be purchased through web advertising companies that will display your ad banner on certain websites for a fixed period of time or to be viewed a specified number of times in various positions on certain popular websites.

■ Chat rooms, discussion lists, bulletin boards and other interactive forums where people of similar interests come together on the Internet to share information are prime places to promote your web-zine. Such sites are the online equivalents of trade shows. With a little research on the Internet, you can usually discover such forums. If one closely related to your topic doesn't exist, it may be worth your while to create one as a means of attracting surfers to your publication.

■ An e-mail subscriber or distribution list can be used to solicit subscribers to your web-zine or e-zine. Lists to which your promotion messages may be e-mailed can be found on the Internet or you can rent them, like a direct-mail list, from Internet marketing companies. Just type in "e-mail lists" on your computer's search line and you'll see the possibilities.

Also, a simple "refer a friend" e-mail link on your web-zine site provides an easy and inexpensive way to have your current subscribers add to your distribution list.

Creating the Online Magazine

The important thing to remember about publishing online magazines is that the only significant difference between them and modern print magazines is the means of distribution. When it comes to creating issues of the magazine, the considerations are virtually the same, whether online or print. Publishers and/or editors of online magazines need to realize that the same skills required for a professional result in print magazines are also required for a professional result in online magazines, since success with the online publication's intended audience, as with those of print magazines, will ultimately depend on readable, relevant, reliable text and attractive display.

The remainder of this book deals with the development of the skills needed to create a quality publication either electronically or in print.

CHAPTER 3

The Editorial Staff and Its Functions

Magazine editorial staffs vary tremendously in size and elaborateness, depending on the following factors: the magazine's editorial concept; the number of editorial pages per issue; the frequency of publication; the magazine's earnings (or its parent organization's revenues, in cases of noncommercial magazines); and the publisher's or owner's willingness to spend money on the product.

Staff functions, however, tend to be the same regardless of the staff's size or the nature of the magazine. There are certain things that must be done to create and produce the issues, and somebody has to do the work, whether the staff is one person or a hundred and one.

It is possible for a magazine to get along with a one-person staff by having the one person—the editor—farm out most of the work to freelance writers, freelance editors, a freelance art director, and freelance photographers and artists. However, in most cases the editor will be working with some sort of staff, which is under his or her supervision and is organized to perform efficiently and well.

Organization of the Staff

Organizing the staff simply means dividing the work and delegating authority to get the work done. The editor of an established magazine will inherit the staff organization already in place, but is often free to modify it. The editor of a start-up magazine or a magazine undergoing radical change is even more likely to feel free to shape the organization of the staff.

Essentially, editorial staffs are organized in two major professional groupings: (1) those who handle the words and (2) those who handle the visual part of the magazine. It's a natural division, for it's a rare person who is good at both words and the visual aspects and who doesn't prefer one over the other. It's to the benefit of the editor and the magazine to have staff members do what they do best and like best.

In addition to the word people and the visual (or art) people, the staff is likely to include support (or clerical) personnel, which on a large magazine could include an office manager, secretaries, typists, clerks and receptionists. On the smallest of magazines, the editor might be expected to handle support tasks himself/herself, typing letters, photocopying, completing forms, filing, ordering supplies, opening mail and so on.

The wise editor who has sufficient resources, however, will organize the staff so that he or she can stay as close as possible to the creative parts of the editor's job and as far as possible from the noncreative parts, such as performing the support tasks or even simply supervising them. One of the best ways to avoid bogging down in support tasks is to have an office manager who is in charge of all the support personnel and all the support problems. The editor remains ultimately responsible, but when it comes to personnel matters concerning the support staff, or problems with office equipment or the building's plumbing or air conditioning or a hundred other things that can commandeer the editor's attention and demand resolution, the editor has one person to turn to and deal with, the office manager. She, or he, as the editor's delegate, worries about such problems, and the editor needs to worry, if worry is appropriate, only about how well the office manager is doing the job.

Included among the staff's word people, on a sizable magazine, would be article editors and editors of certain special subjects or departments or features. The main job of those editors is to conceive, acquire and process editorial content. Also included would be writers—whose job is writing titles and subtitles, captions, blurbs, shorts, the table of contents, cover lines, certain standing features and sometimes full-size articles—and copy editors, who do research and fact-checking as well as copy editing and proofreading.

The art people would include: the art director, or design director; perhaps an associate or assistant art director; a photo editor, or director of photography; perhaps assistant photo editors if it's a large magazine that uses a lot of photographs; graphic artists who create illustrations on computers or otherwise; and layout artists, who make up the pages, using computers and scanners. The larger the magazine—more pages, more material—the larger the staff needed to do the work.

All editorial staff members ordinarily are directly responsible to the editor. Magazines with large staffs may have a more elaborate hierarchy, with certain low-level staffers being responsible to certain higher-level staffers and those higher-level staffers being directly responsible to the editor.

Some magazines designate certain staffers to be in charge of certain issues of the magazine. Those people often are called issue editors and they work much like *the* editor on the issues for which they are responsible, perhaps three or four or six a year. Issue editors work under the authority of the editor, who appoints them and gives them, more or less, a free hand, but reserves the right to overrule them and redirect them at any stage of an issue's development. The issue-editor system is a way of sharing the editor's burden on a large magazine that publishes a lot of material, such as *Reader's Digest*, which uses the system. On small magazines with relatively small staffs and only a dozen or so articles per issue, it usually isn't necessary or even desirable.

Roles and Requirements of the Editor

No matter how elaborate or how simple the staff organization is, the editor's job is always complex, comprising a range of duties and demanding a variety of abilities. The job calls for a person who can fulfill half a dozen roles. Specifically, the ideal editor is:

Creator

Issues of the magazine must be created—and created from material and illustration that also must be created. The editor is the person with the ultimate responsibility for creating the editorial product, issue by issue. Thus the editor's job is, above all else, a job of creating, constantly creating.

Representative Reader

The material that goes into the magazine and the way the material is presented must satisfy the readers. The readers must be interested in what the magazine offers them. To successfully edit the magazine, the editor must know what the readers want, what they need, what interests them, how to talk to them. The editor must think the way the readers think. She, or he, must be the authentic representative of the magazine's readers.

Creative Director

Not only must the editor be a creator herself; she must inspire and lead the creative efforts of the rest of the magazine's staff—editors, writers, art director, photo editor. Working through the art director and photo editor, the editor must also be able to lead the creative efforts of freelance photographers and illustrators. And when there's conflict—which there's very likely to be occasionally—the editor must be the arbiter, judging, then delivering the final word.

Policymaker

The editor is usually the last word on how things are to be done, whether it's a matter of style, compensation to freelancers, a search for a new staff member, submission of manuscripts, editorial meetings or any of a couple hundred other things that require wise and consistent decisions or responses.

Conductor

One of the biggest challenges of the editor's job is to get from each of the assorted staff members the very best that's in them. The staff, ideally, is composed of individuals with different talents and temperaments, and the editor is the person who gets them to work together, leading, coordinating, harmonizing and sometimes adjudicating their efforts. The staff is the orchestra; the editor is the conductor; the magazine is the music.

Manager

The editor must be the manager not merely of the magazine but of the editorial department. An office manager can lighten the load significantly, but in the end it's the editor who is responsible (and accountable) to the publisher or owner of the magazine. That means the editor must manage people, both creative and clerical, and money (especially) as well as time, space, equipment, supplies and every other resource used by the department. (For more on the editor as a manager, see Chapter 4.)

To perform well in those roles, the editor needs to come equipped with certain abilities and skills, or acquire them as he goes along. The person who is the editor must:

1. Be something of a writer. The editor need not be a great writer himself, but he needs to be enough of a writer to know good writing from bad and know how to make good from bad. He, or she, should have enough experience at writing magazine pieces to understand standard reporting and writing problems and be able to offer practical and psychological help to the magazine's writers, freelancers and staffers alike.

2. Be a wordsmith. The editor needs to know the language and appreciate the precision of words. He ought to be a word craftsman, working with words—whether in text or titles or wherever else in the magazine—in the same way a master woodworker chooses and works with his tools. He must stubbornly insist that writers and editors use the right word in the right place—and spell it correctly.

3. Have an eye for illustration and design. The editor who shows little interest in, or facility for, anything but words will be only half an editor. The words—the text of the content—must be displayed and presented to the reader in an attractive, interest-arresting way. The editor should not be neutral or opinionless about how the text will be displayed and presented to the reader. Turning the look of the magazine completely over to the art director is a mistake to be avoided. The editor, ideally, should be thinking about illustration while thinking of the pieces themselves, if not in the planning stage at least in the editing stage. Ideally, the editor should be able to visualize the piece in the magazine. While issues are still in the planning stages the editor must be able to recognize wrong illustration and poor design—and, when it occurs, insist on something better, offering ideas of his own when necessary.

4. Understand the audience. If the audience is automobile seat-cover manufacturers, the editor has to know what they think about and what they want to know about. If the audience is junior high school girls, the editor has to know what *they* think about and what they're interested in. Many editors, particularly on trade magazines and special-interest consumer magazines, have to learn their audience before they can fully learn their jobs.

5. Show enthusiasm. Enthusiasm, in the words of Norman Vincent Peale, the great popularizer of positive thinking, makes the difference. The editor needs to know that if the magazine's staff is going to perform at its best, it must be enthusiastic about what it is doing and enthusiastic about the publication. Enthusiasm about putting the magazine together and about the magazine itself begins with the editor and spreads to the staff through her, or him. Enthusiasm is contagious. The editor must feel it and show it.

6. Apply tact in directing others. The editor should be striving for excellence in every piece, every issue. To get it, he sometimes must prod staff members to give him what he wants for the magazine. He must get others to give him what he wants without having to order it done, without crushing, humiliating or antagonizing the staff member. The editor must always be sensitive to the feelings of the magazine's staff members and use tact to achieve desired results in the magazine. Coercion should always be the absolutely last resort.

Staffers who are consistently overruled, whose opinions are consistently rejected, are bound eventually to become demoralized and disaffected—a situation the editor must guard against if he or she wants the staff to continue to perform effectively. Everyone needs a victory once in awhile, and creative people probably need it more than most. The editor needs to remember that he doesn't have to always be right. He can afford to let someone else be right sometimes, even when he knows the other person is wrong.

The important thing for the editor is to be right when it really matters. When it doesn't really matter, someone else can be right. The editor has to know when to insist and when to yield.

7. Be articulate. If the editor is to win staff members over to her view, her way of doing it, she will have to be not only tactful but articulate. She needs to be able to express her opinions and ideas so that others, staffers and freelancers alike, see and understand and therefore can deliver what she wants.

The power of clear and persuasive speech is also essential when the editor deals with other parts of the company or parent organization. When dealing with the publisher or owner, for example, the editor must be able to represent the magazine and herself well and must be able to present her or the magazine's case effectively.

8. Have common sense. To make the decisions that the editor must make in producing a quality piece of journalism (or public relations), there is simply no good substitute for common sense. Intelligence, education, talent, energy—nothing takes the place of feet-firmly-on-the-ground horse sense. Common sense helps the editor recognize baloney when he sees or hears it and helps make him impervious to it, which he should be, in all its forms.

9. *Be (or become) a manager as well as an editor.* The editor must know or be able to quickly learn some of the same management principles and skills necessary for managers of other kinds of enterprises. The editor must be or become skillful particularly in the areas of planning, budgeting and fiscal management. (See Chapter 4 for more on the editor as manager.)

Roles and Requirements of the Art Director

The editor's chief aide and partner in the making of magazines is the art director. Generally the editor can handle whatever needs to be handled in the word part of the magazine. What she needs help with—expert help—is the visual part of the magazine. The editor's bag is words; the art director is the visual expert.

Because the work of the art director is so vital to the magazine, so important to its success, the editor must have an art director with whom she is compatible—which is the first requirement for an art director. The art director should share the editor's tastes (or vice versa) in illustration, in layout and in the overall appearance of the magazine. The art director who cannot or will not give the editor what he or she wants needs to move or be moved to another job. Life is too short to spend it hassling with an art director. The editor must have an art director whose ideas and preferences naturally mesh with the editor's own.

Other than being the editor's and the magazine's visual expert, the art director has four major functions:

Visual Creator

The art director is responsible for what the magazine's readers see, as opposed to what they read. The art director creates the look of the magazine, piece by piece and issue by issue. She or he designs the editorial pages (the pages on which text appears), down to the smallest detail. She determines or helps determine what is to be included in photographs and artwork, the size and shape of photos and artwork, how many photos or pieces of artwork are or can be included with the text and which photos are to be published, which are not.

The editors create the magazine's words; the art director creates the look of the magazine.

Procurer of Photographers and Illustrators

Magazines generally use freelance photographers and illustrators (people who are not members of the staff or employees of the company), and it is the art director's job to find suitable ones. It is also the art director, or the photo editor if there is one, working with the art director, who makes the photo and art assignments, whether to a freelancer or a staffer.

In cases where existing photographs or artwork illustrations are to be used in the magazine, the art director is responsible for acquiring them.

Production Expert

As an architect must know not only design but construction, the art director must know not only design but the graphic arts. The editor must understand, but the art director especially must understand the steps of production that take layouts and type from the magazine's offices to the printer's plant and eventually to the readers' hands. The art director must know how to make what he sees in his head come out of the printing press. That means she or he must be especially skilled in desktop publishing and knowledgeable about the use of color, among other things.

The art director also often functions as the editor's chief adviser in all matters concerning production.

Manager

The art director is ordinarily the head of the magazine's art department and as such must have the same people, money and planning skills as the editor. The larger the art department, of course, the greater the need for administrative ability. Even in a one-person art department, however, the art director is still a manager, managing freelance photographers and illustrators and the art department's budget allocation.

In all aspects of her job, the art director is responsible to the editor, and major decisions involving the art department are, or should be, made only with the editor's approval.

The Masthead and How to Use It

Ordinarily the names of members of the magazine's professional staff, and sometimes one or more of the key support personnel, are listed in the masthead, generally in a descending order of authority and status. The masthead is several things. It is, first of all, the staff's table of organization, showing how the staff is organized. It's also the *Who's Who* of the editorial department. And perhaps most revealing of all, it defines the staff's pecking order. A wise editor will realize the significance of the masthead and the importance that staff members attach to it.

It's the editor, of course, who determines who is included in the masthead, the staff member's title (associate editor, assistant editor, editorial assistant and so forth) and the position of the staff member's name in the masthead. The editor therefore can use the masthead as a system of rewards. Mere inclusion on the masthead, for example, can be a reward for the newcomer who proves him or herself after a trial period on the magazine. A new title and a higher position on the masthead can sometimes be almost as effective as a pay raise as a way to recognize a staffer's good work. A new, grander title and upward movement in the masthead are things that the editor can give to a deserving staffer when there's nothing in the editorial budget to give.

The wise editor will use the masthead to help motivate the staff and to give recognition for increased responsibility and jobs well done.

CHAPTER 4

Managing the Editorial Department

B esides performing the creative tasks of an editor, the magazine's editor must also *manage*. As head of the editorial department, the editor must manage the functions of the people, the resources and the processes needed to produce the magazine. The aspiring editor in chief must be aware that there's more to his or her job than the purely editorial parts, and ideally he or she will go to the editor in chief's job knowing how to be a successful manager, regardless of the size or nature of the magazine or of the company or organization that publishes the magazine. The editor in chief must be, or become, a successful manager.

What Is a Manager?

A manager is a person with many roles—administrator, planner, organizer, director, controller and, in some instances, policeman. He is responsible for efficiently accomplishing the mission of whatever organization he works for. In many cases the organization that publishes the magazine is a business venture, intended to make a profit. In other cases the magazine is published by an educational institution, a foundation or a religious organization. In any case, the functions of the editor as a manager are likely to be the same.

As manager, the editor is responsible for securing resources and doing so within the organization's rules. The editor is also responsible for planning and coordinating the functions of the editorial department with other departments of the organization, such as advertising and circulation, as well as with outside agencies, such as the color separator, the printer and freelance contributors.

Another vital part of the job of editor as manager is serving as the liaison between the editorial department's workers and the decision-making unit of the organization. For commercial magazines, the decision-making unit is usually the publisher. For other kinds of magazines it may be the organization's president or its vice president for public relations.

Depending on the size, complexity and centralization of the organization that publishes the magazine, members of the magazine's staff might be far removed from the organization's decision-making process. In organizations that grant some autonomy to their employees, on the other hand, editorial department workers might be directly involved in decision-making. Having an influence on decision-making can be extremely important for staff members, particularly when worker benefits such as medical insurance, the company's pension plan, vacations and leave time are being affected.

As liaison with the powers that be, the editor owes responsibilities to the magazine's staff members and, at the same time, to the organization's top management. The responsibilities are the same no matter the nature or size of the magazine.

Responsibilities to the Staff

The editor is likely to be responsible for decisions on hiring, promotion, job assignment and firing within the editorial department. He, or she, might also have to act as the company's mediator in employee disputes and may have to act as a disciplinarian over errant editorial department workers.

The editor is also the employees' link to the top of the organization. He or she should be the staff's representative and its voice in expressing staff members' concerns to higher-ups.

Responsibilities to Management

The editor is the person who is responsible for the editorial staff's part in accomplishing the mission of the organization and is accountable to higher-level administrators in the organization. The editor must be deeply concerned with the functioning of the editorial department and must also remain aware of how the editorial department fits into the overall functioning of the company or other organization. The editor must act as a boundary spanner and be responsive to the need for integration and coordination of the editorial department with other parts of the organization.

The Importance of Effective Management

If organizations were machines and organization workers were machine parts, a manager's job would be merely to turn the machine on in the morning and off at the end of the day. The manager would dictate the desired output, and the machine would produce it efficiently and ceaselessly during operation. Occasionally a part might break or the entire machine might require a tune-up, and the manager would replace the part or secure the needed maintenance. The manager's job would be that of an engineer.

But organizations are not machines, and workers do not behave like machine parts. Workers are individuals and have varying feelings, needs, motives and abilities. Within any organization, including a magazine's editorial department, because the workers are humans, there are likely to be crises, conflicts and other problems arising continuously. It's the job of the editor, as manager, to face and resolve those problems.

A manager's main role, in fact, is essentially that of a problem-solver. When problems—the seriousness of which may range from the seemingly trivial to the obviously critical—arise, the ultimate responsibility for resolution falls on the appropriate manager. If the problem is in the editorial department, it might, and in some cases should, be resolved by a subeditor—the chief copy editor, for example—or by the art director, depending on the nature of the problem and how much authority the editor has delegated to key staffers. But the editor nevertheless is responsible for resolving everyday problems and doing so with the organization's best interests, as defined by top management, clearly in mind.

The editor's job as manager requires smoothing out the everyday functions of the editorial department. The smoothing out can include securing a staff adequate to produce the magazine well and on time, adjusting the payroll to encourage or at least adequately compensate individual staff members, and maintaining good relations with other parts of the organization by spanning the boundaries and making sure that barriers to the editorial staff's performance are avoided or removed. Those barriers can include: the workspace allotted to the editorial department; the editorial department's equipment and software; the supplies needed by staff members; and the setting of editorial deadlines by the advertising department, the circulation department or the production department.

The editor must be a manager who effectively handles the people in the editorial department, the workers who are under his authority. In addition, he or she must successfully handle the people elsewhere in the organization. Some of those people can, by design or incidentally, affect the performance of the editor or other members of the magazine's staff. The editor's success and the success of the magazine, to a great extent, depend on how effective the editor is as a manager.

Principles of Good Management

One key to successful managing is foresight. The successful manager is one who doesn't merely react to and resolve problems once they arise but who forestalls problems from arising in the first place. A good driver is not necessarily one who time and again swerves or brakes to avoid accidents at the last second; rather the good driver is one who foresees the potential for a mishap and avoids it before an emergency arises.

To head off problems before they arise, a manager needs a clear view of the road ahead. She must be able to anticipate likely obstacles before she gets to them. Through planning, looking ahead and knowing what adjustments can be made and safeguards be taken to avoid the obstacles, an effective editor can guide the magazine's staff expeditiously past the obstructions without costly delays or diminished quality. When extraordinary circumstances arise and threaten missed deadlines or compromises in the editorial product, the editor should fall back on contingency plans or quickly decide on an alternative course of action.

Another key to successful managing is leadership. To be an effective manager, the editor, like any other manager, must become a leader. At first glance, "manager" and "leader" might seem to be the same thing, but there are important distinctions between the two roles. A person can be a manager but not a leader, and the opposite is true as well. The functions of a leader generally relate to the *human* side of an organization, rather than the assets, the systems or the procedures of the organization. The editor, as leader of the editorial staff, is concerned with motivating, supporting and influencing the members of the editorial staff and in fostering within staff members a sense of commitment—to the editor, to the magazine and to the purposes of the company or other organization.

Good management and leadership require good communication. As manager, the editor must become a skillful communicator, realizing that effective communication is a two-way process. The editor must be good not only at clearly relaying information and instructions to staff members, both professional and clerical, and to freelancers as well, but must also be good at listening to the information and signals that come from people in the organization who occupy positions above, below or next to the editor.

In order to get the best from the magazine's staff members, the editor must know when to wield power and when not to. The editor needs power to get things done, just like a car needs gas to keep it going.

Part of an editor's power comes from the position he or she holds. The position of editor, regardless of who occupies it, has authority vested in it by the organization. The editor, for example, has the power to reward staffers by giving raises, bonuses, days off, desirable assignments and promotions. The editor also has the power to reprimand, reassign or fire.

That "position" power also gives the editor some degree of discretion in directing activities within the editorial department. When an exception to a rule needs to be made or circumstances arise that haven't been encountered before, the editor must assess whether she has the power to act on that problem. Depending on the power given to the editor from the organization, there will be guidelines within which he or she can make, break or change rules within the editorial department. An effective editor will know the bounds within which he or she can and cannot work. Likewise, an effective editor will establish boundaries for and empower the magazine's staff members.

Personal power is another source of power an editor should develop and use over followers. Personal power comes from the characteristics of the person filling the position and is granted by the followers, rather than by the organization. Respect and admiration are the cornerstones of personal power. An editor who is seen as someone worth listening to and following will bring about greater levels of staff commitment and enthusiasm than an editor who must rely exclusively on threats and bribes—position power only.

If an editor's personal power erodes or fails to emerge, he or she should take steps to build the trust and respect of the staffers. Otherwise, the editor will have to encourage performance by using his or her position power alone. A leader is someone whom the followers perceive as worthy of following, not merely obeying. Personal power forms the foundation for leadership.

Leader power, like power in a car battery, must be drawn on to make things happen. A car will not start, even with a charged battery, until the power of the battery is tapped. A combination of powers—personal and position—can be used to encourage or make the followers comply with the editor's requests.

If the power of the car battery is too weak, the car will not start. Likewise, if the power of the battery is too strong and incompatible with the car's electrical system, the car will not start. An appropriate amount of power is needed to bring about optimal performance. The same is true for human systems. The leader who doesn't have enough power, or doesn't draw on it, will not encourage performance from the followers. Similarly, the leader who abuses or misuses power will also see performance suffer—perhaps eventually leading to sparks and fire.

An effective editor will be able to bring out high performance from staff members, both professional and clerical, and from freelancers as well. To perform, a person must have desire and ability. When the staff member's "want to" and "able to" are correctly matched, performance will occur. When performance problems arise in subordinates, the editor must be quick to identify whether it is the result of a problem with motivation or with ability or a combination of the two. Once the problem has been assessed, the manager must implement solutions.

When an ability problem exists, there is no point in trying to enhance the motivation of the subordinate without also addressing the ability problem. No matter how motivated a man might be to flap his arms and become airborne, he doesn't have the ability to fly. Likewise, when a highly capable, experienced person is not performing up to his or her potential, the ability of that staffer is probably not the cause of the problem. If a car's fuel system is causing poor performance, it does no good to spend time and effort correcting the car's suspension. The solution needs to fit the problem.

How to Handle Motivation Problems

When a performance problem arises from staffers not wanting to perform (a motivation problem), there are several things the editor should assess. A staff member may not want to perform for one or more of a host of possible reasons. Perhaps he is bored with the task, which may by its nature be uninteresting. Maybe the staffer doesn't see why the task needs to be done; maybe she feels that she won't get anything for, or out of, accomplishing the task, or that the payoff is something she doesn't care about.

Those are possibilities the editor should consider when trying to fix, improve or maintain staff motivation. Different kinds of motivation problems require different solutions—each specifically devised for the person and the situation in which the problem exists. Solutions to motivation problems may be as simple as the editor's explaining the importance of the task in the overall workings of the department. Reassigning tasks or increasing job responsibilities may also solve some motivation problems.

The rewards that a staff member gains from successful completion of the task are also important in effecting optimal performance. Some staffers will receive high levels of internal satisfaction from accomplishing a task; others may be driven by purely external rewards, such as money, status or perquisites. The effective leader must be aware of what it is that drives his or her followers and offer those rewards for effort and performance.

Desirable rewards must be linked to performance. Whether the reward is a pat on the back, public recognition, a promotion or a pay raise, it must be perceived as being associated with effort and performance. Motivation is weakened when no rewards are given for performance and when rewards are given for non-performance. Both the desirability of the rewards and the fairness of the manner in which they are distributed must be assessed by the editor.

How to Handle Ability Problems

When performance problems stem from an inability to perform, the editor must assess a variety of personal and situational characteristics. Does the staff member know how to do the task? Does he or she have the resources needed to carry out the task? Is the task impossible for the staffer to perform? Are there characteristics of the organization or environment that hinder performance?

Some ability problems in staffers can be handled by the editor; others might require assistance from higher-ups in the organization. Others might require a change in the environment, and some may be impossible to solve. Training, retraining or reassignment of individuals to another position may solve some skills problems among staff members.

Resource problems that affect ability might require the editor to acquire materials, equipment, money or space from elsewhere in the organization or even outside the organization. Some resource problems may arise from the editorial department's being too dependent on other departments in the organization. If the advertising department is slow in passing ad schedules to the editorial department, for example, performance of some editorial staffers might suffer. In such cases, the editor/manager may have to seek help from higher-ranking officials to solve the problem.

Some resource problems may be out of the control of either the editor or the organization. Laws, governmental regulations, economic conditions or other things may present ability problems for the editorial department. Sometimes resource problems are unsolvable—and it is then up to the editor to choose an appropriate course of action to cope with the difficulty.

An effective manager/leader/editor will be able to assess performance problems and determine how the motivation and ability of the staff members, both professional and clerical, can be fine-tuned to achieve optimal performance.

Management Pitfalls and How to Avoid Them

Like any other manager, the editor will face a variety of perils that go with the job. The prudent editor will be alert to any danger that interferes with the performance of his job, but he will be especially aware of those to which he is most likely to be susceptible. On the path to successful management, the most common pitfalls are lost respect, misuse of power, isolation and burnout.

Lost Respect

The biggest pitfall of management is a leader's separation from the followers. When a manager becomes cold and aloof to the needs of the followers, he or she will lose their respect and their commitment to the manager, and possibly to the entire enterprise. A manager must work at maintaining a leader image in the eyes of the followers.

The ability to lead—rather than merely to boss—is dependent on the willing subordination of the followers. A leader must be seen by the followers as actually being their leader. He or she must be perceived as representing the values and ideals of the followers. The magazine's editor must be perceived by the staff as wanting the same things for the magazine and for the staff as the staff members themselves want.

When a leader ceases to represent the followers' ideals, she in turn loses her leader status. When the editor no longer holds, or no longer seems to hold, the values of her staff, the staff will not see her as their leader, but only their boss. They will then comply with the editor's wishes, requests and instructions only to the extent that the leader has position power over them and can formally require their compliance.

To avoid this pitfall, the editor who leads his or her staff—instead of merely bossing them—must by word and deed reaffirm the staffers' values, must show that he cares about the same things the staff members care about. The editor must maintain open relations with the staff members, must be accessible to them, and must listen to them.

It is vital for any leader—and particularly a magazine editor, who depends on the creativity and cooperation of the magazine's staff—to understand and represent the needs and interests of the followers. The editor must keep focused not merely on the job of creating and producing issues of the magazine but on the people who help get the job done.

Misuse of Power

Nothing or no one will destroy the motivation and morale of subordinates more surely or more quickly than a leader who abuses his or her power. Managers who use their formal position power to threaten and coerce subordinates will gain from their followers neither devotion to the job nor loyalty to the manager or to the organization.

Wise leaders, instead of misusing their authority, use it to empower their followers. "Empowerment" means giving power to the followers. The magazine's staff members should be responsible, in part, for making decisions, devising solutions and implementing those solutions. Empowerment can bring about feelings of self-worth and importance in the followers. When followers have a part in the decision-making process, they are more likely to follow through in the application of the solutions.

Followers should be allowed to take credit for their successes. Failure, however, should be shared between the followers and the leader. If failure is punished, risks will not be taken, and innovation will not occur. For a magazine, the loss of innovation is likely to mean the diminution of creativity, which is the lifeblood of successful magazines.

Empowerment means giving power to the followers—it does not mean abdicating power. The leader makes sure the followers have the requisite abilities and resources to accomplish their tasks. The leader also makes sure the followers have a clear understanding of their goal. After that, the empowered staff members have autonomy to develop the means to the ends. It is the leader, however, who defines the ends.

Although the editor gives some of his authority to certain staff members, the ultimate responsibility remains with the editor. No matter how much the staff members are empowered, no matter how much authority the editor delegates, it is the editor who remains responsible for the magazine and the staff that produces it.

Isolation

If the manager becomes consumed with his position in the organization, or the position of his or her unit in the organization, the entire organizational system can be thrown out of kilter. Just as the organs in the human body work together to carry out the functions of the body, so do the components and subsystems within an organization. When a component of the body's system is out of kilter with the other components, the entire body slows down and loses some effectiveness in its functioning.

As manager, the editor must assess the effectiveness of the editorial department *and* must also assess, through communication with other parts of the organization, how the editorial department needs to perform in relation to the other parts of the organization.

At times it may be necessary for the editorial department to back off from optimal performance in order for the entire organization to perform at its best. A star football running back who outruns his linemen's blocking assignments will not be as effective as one who slows down enough to let his linemen do their jobs before he goes all out. The manager of an editorial department that turns out magazines without regard for what is going on in the advertising, circulation and promotion departments, for example, runs the risk of messing up the total plan and making enemies elsewhere in the organization at the same time.

Coordination and integration with other parts of the organization are needed for the good of the organization, not to mention the success of the manager. The editor, whether of a commercial magazine, a public relations magazine or some other kind of publication, needs to avoid living only in his own little editorial world. Success as editor, as head of the editorial department, depends on the editor's ability to thrive in the *total world* of the organization.

Burnout

The editor, just like any other professional manager, is subject to eventual burnout. Deadlines, meetings, production problems, employee problems, freelance problems and problems with the organization's top management all create stress for the editor. Encountered day to day, year after year, the job's stress can eventually injure, even destroy, a person both physically and mentally.

Stress is not necessarily bad, however. It often is the motivator that gets us up and performing. But in excess, it can disrupt a person's physical and mental processes and thereby harm performance. Planning, delegating, reassigning or redesigning tasks and effectively managing one's time are some ways that an editor/manager can handle or eliminate some everyday stressors on the job.

Maintaining a balanced lifestyle, staying in good physical condition, staying mentally healthy and having a social network of supportive people to talk with are several ways of increasing one's capacity to cope with stress. Vacations and time away from work are also effective weapons in combating the ever-present stresses that a managerial position entails.

Conclusion

Complex systems require coordination mechanisms. In human work systems, including a magazine-publishing enterprise, that coordination mechanism is the manager. The manager is responsible for a vast array of activities and duties. In addition to being responsible for the performance of many different duties, the manager is responsible to many different people. The manager is the tool that the organization uses to turn its goals into reality.

For managing an editorial staff to produce issues of a magazine, the indispensable organizational tool is the editor, and to do his job well, he must be a wise manager as well as a wise editor.

CHAPTER 5

Acquiring the Content

For most magazines, the *word* is the thing.

With the obvious exception of skin magazines, and some others, a magazine's text is the big reason readers buy and read the magazine. To the readers, the editorial content *is* the magazine. Lavish photography spectacularly reproduced helps mightily to dress up the magazine and attract readers, but when a potential reader is finished flipping the pages and browsing through the magazine, it's the stuff listed in the table of contents that really counts.

Of all the responsibilities a magazine's editor bears, none is so weighty or constant as acquiring the content. It is the editor's Job No. 1. Getting good, relevant, reliable, readable words into the magazine, issue after issue, is the quintessence of the editor's responsibility.

The appropriateness and relevance of the content's subjects (tennis, personal computers, rock music, the state of Maine or whatever else the readers expect to read about) naturally vary from magazine to magazine, depending on the magazine's editorial concept and its audience. But the ways to *acquire* editorial content are practically universal, regardless of subject, regardless of audience. Knowing them is absolutely vital to the editor's success.

Kinds of Content

Magazines generally thrive on variety—variety in subject, tone, length and illustration potential of the pieces of content. The editor must be careful to keep the magazine's inventory stocked with a range of pieces, making sure there are always enough different kinds of content to put a proper mix into each issue.

A magazine's mainstay, of course, is the full-size article, usually running from about 2,000 words in length to about 5,000. In addition, the content might include: standing features (pieces that are on the same general topic or set of topics, or by the same writer, and that run each issue, or at least regularly, and usually under the same title or head); two-pagers (pieces contained on two pages in the magazine, usually on a spread), one-pagers (pieces contained on a single page in the magazine), picture stories (accompanied by text blocks or fat captions), editorials, departments, essays, columns, lists, letters, shorts and whatever else serves the readers' interest. (The term "short" is more apt than "filler," since "filler" may suggest a piece of content placed into the magazine merely to fill out a page, while a short is planned for and *scheduled* into the magazine, usually for the sake of variety.)

Where the Content Comes From

The editor can draw material from an array of sources and he or she should learn to use them all. The major sources:

■ *The staff.* Most ideas for articles and other content come from staff members, especially the editor himself/herself, who ought to know better than anyone else what the readers want, what he wants for the readers and what the magazine should have in it.

Ideas that the editor decides are worth pursuing are then assigned, either to a staffer or to a freelance writer. (A freelance writer is not necessarily someone who makes a living freelancing, but is anyone who is not a staff member—nor otherwise connected with the magazine—and who writes for the magazine, once or once in a while or regularly.)

■ *Queries from freelancers.* Some ideas for content will come as written queries from freelancers. If the editor decides an idea from a freelancer is worth pursuing, she may make an assignment to that freelancer.

■ *Unsolicited manuscripts.* Almost any magazine that has been in business awhile, particularly if it's a consumer magazine, receives unsolicited material. Unsolicited pieces, also called "slush" or "over the transom" pieces, are written either by the magazine's readers or by freelancers (or would-be freelancers) who, instead of querying the editor to find out if the magazine has any interest in the piece, goes ahead and writes it, then sends it in and hopes for the best. It's common for big consumer magazines to be flooded with unsolicited pieces, precious few of which prove usable.

A magazine's own staff members submit unsolicited pieces sometimes, in the same way a freelancer does. The editor usually will want to make sure those pieces get a considerate reading and, if they are not acceptable for publication, a gentle rejection that encourages the staffer to try again sometime.

Unsolicited manuscripts also occasionally come from literary agents—a circumstance that does not necessarily mean those pieces are any better than those that come directly from freelancers.

The editor can't depend on unsolicited material to provide the magazine with any particular quantity, not to mention quality, of content. But some magazines find enough gems there to make continued reading of unsolicited material worth their while.

■ *Reprints.* These are articles or other pieces that have been published in another publication.

■ *Excerpts.* Some books are suitable for excerpting, yielding a chapter or so that can be neatly lifted out of the book to make a magazine article.

■ *Condensations. Reader's Digest* is famous for compressing virtually an entire book into a piece the size of a long article and running it in the magazine. Other magazines also have used book condensations, running them either as one long piece or as a serial in consecutive issues.

Generating Ideas for Content

Unlike newspaper stories, which usually begin with an event, magazine pieces begin with an idea. And unlike newspaper editors, who can go to their wire services and syndicated features to fill an edition if necessary, magazine editors, with a special audience and a specific editorial concept, must look to their own resources to provide material for their magazines' pages. For most magazines the continual conception of story ideas, the month-to-month spawning of new content, is critically important, and it's the business of the editor to make sure the ideas keep coming.

A magazine's richest and most dependable source of ideas is (or should be) the magazine's staff. The magazine's editor should be the *chief* generator of ideas, particularly on small magazines, but every staff member is expected to contribute ideas. The staff should be a fountain from which a steady stream of good, usable story ideas continuously flows. If there are staffers who are *not* offering ideas, they ought to be told that they are expected to do so. Young staffers may be unaware that they are supposed to be not merely processors of material, but *inventors* of material.

If they don't already know, the editor should also tell staff members *how* to submit ideas—as a memo to the editor or to some other staff member, as an oral presentation (made from a written memo that can be turned over to the editor) at a staff meeting, as e-mail sent to certain members of the staff, or however else the editor wants it done. Whatever the method, all staff members should offer a certain minimum number of ideas per week, per month or per meeting. The editor will let his staff members know what he expects, and those staffers who consistently originate pieces that make their way into the magazine should be rewarded and treasured by the grateful editor.

How to Work with Freelancers

There are several situations in which the editor works with freelance writers:

■ *Unsolicited manuscripts.* The editor or the magazine's publisher (because it's a time-and-money matter) must decide whether the magazine will consider unsolicited material. If the answer is yes, it's a good idea to publish in each issue a notice spelling out how submissions are to be made and emphasizing that a self-addressed, stamped envelope must be included with the manuscript if the author wants it returned.

If the editor likes the idea of the piece but not the piece itself, as submitted, she should not feel it is being offered on a take-it-or-leave-it basis. Instead, she should tell the author what needs to be done to make the piece something the magazine would consider. When suggesting a revision of an unsolicited manuscript, the editor must be specific, but need not promise the author anything except a careful and interested rereading of the piece if the revision is made.

Unsolicited manuscripts will get one of three possible replies after being considered: (1) "We like it and we're going to buy it"; (2) "It's not something for us, and we're returning it herewith"; or (3) "We think it has possibilities, and if you will revise it as follows, we would be happy to have another look at it." If after revision the piece meets the editor's approval, the new reply is No. 1; if not, the new reply is No. 2.

Unsolicited pieces that show that the author probably could write a successful piece, even though the present one is not acceptable, should get a personal reply from the editor or one of the magazine's other staff editors, letting the author down gently and inviting him to try again sometime.

Pieces that are unacceptable and fail to indicate that the author might do better in the future may be returned with a form rejection notice, assuming the author has sent along a self-addressed, stamped envelope.

■ *Queries.* The one big rule about queries is that they must be *written*—except in the most extraordinary, most urgent cases.

There are at least three good reasons for the editor to require written queries. One is that an idea may have to pass before more than one set of eyes before it's approved. A telephone query, to be considered by more than one editor, would have to be redescribed orally or put in writing by the staff member who talked to the querying author. The burden of presentation of the idea should fall on the querying author, not the staff member.

Another reason is that the written query provides a sample of the prospective author's writing ability. It shows whether the author can present material in an organized, logical sequence. It shows if he can recognize good material when he finds it and knows what to do with it when he's got it.

Still another reason is that the written query shows whether the prospective author is a writer, not merely a talker. The editor should be wary of the writer who talks a great story but, when it comes to putting words on paper, is permanently out to lunch. If a prospective author can't or won't put his idea down in a written query, chances are he can't or won't deliver a manuscript either.

The query should vividly describe the piece that the querying author is proposing. If it doesn't, the reason is probably that the querying author doesn't see the piece clearly himself, which is a warning signal to the editor. The query should offer some of the material the proposed piece will contain—specific numbers, documentation, quotes, some descriptive detail and even an anecdote or two. The editor should get not only a clear idea of the proposed piece but a clear idea of the querying author's potential for reporting and writing the piece. If he doesn't, that's another warning signal.

So the editor's rejection of a query might result from an article idea that's a poor idea, or at least a poor one for his magazine, but it might result, too, from an imprecise description or an otherwise faulty presentation of the idea. The editor must feel certain about the idea *and* the author before giving him a go-ahead.

If the editor is sold on both counts, she may give the querying author an assignment to write the piece he is proposing. However, if the editor is sold on only one of the two counts, she might do less than assign the proposed piece. If the idea proposed is not exactly the way the editor believes a piece on that subject should be written for her magazine's audience, but she is persuaded the querying author *can* do the piece, she can change the angle and put the revised idea up to the author; and if he agrees to it, *then* she will make the assignment.

Or if the editor likes the idea but has doubts about the querying author's ability to deliver the proposed piece, she can suggest he do the piece on speculation (or "spec"), which means the editor encourages the writer to do the piece and submit it to the magazine but the magazine does not promise the writer anything other than an interested reading. The editor, in that way, does not commit the magazine for a fee or expenses. If the querying author does the piece and the editor finds it acceptable, then of course the magazine would pay the author the usual fee and, to do the right thing, would reimburse him for reasonable expenses incurred in reporting and writing the piece.

■ *Finder's fees.* There's another way of compensating a querying author for producing less than a usable piece. If the editor likes the idea but does not want to give the querying author the assignment (because she's skeptical about his writing ability or she doubts he can get access to the material, or because the freelancer would have to travel across the country to see the sources and thus run up a prohibitive expense bill), the editor can thank the querying author and pay him a finder's fee, usually a small fraction of the magazine's ordinary fee for an article. The querying author wouldn't have to do anything else and would still get a check.

The editor then assigns the story to a more dependable writer and/or one who lives near the story's sources. That way, the editor increases the chances of getting a usable piece and getting it at a reasonable price, including expenses.

■ *Assignments.* The best deal for a freelancer is to write the piece on assignment from the magazine. An assignment means the magazine has: commissioned the freelancer to report and write the piece; promised to pay a specific amount if the piece is successful; probably agreed to pay the writer's legitimate expenses; and probably promised to pay the freelancer a guarantee—also called a "kill fee"— in case the piece fails. Doing a piece on assignment has, for the freelancer, several advantages over writing an unsolicited piece. With an unsolicited piece, the freelancer researches the story at his expense, writes it at a cost of his time, and finally sends it in with only a hope that the magazine will be interested in it. An assignment also has advantages for the freelancer over doing the piece on speculation, since the freelancer on assignment is ordinarily promised reimbursement for reasonable expenses and a kill fee if the piece bombs, whereas doing it on spec he is promised nothing but an interested reading.

The assignment's advantages to the magazine are of a lesser scale, but there are some. To the editor an assignment means (1) the freelancer has agreed to write the piece that the editor wants, (2) the freelancer has promised to write the piece according to the editor's specifications and (3) the freelancer has promised to deliver the piece within a certain amount of time. An assignment does not mean, however, that those promises will be kept.

An assignment might come as a result of the freelancer's having conceived the idea for the piece and queried the magazine, or as a result of the magazine's having originated the idea and picked the particular freelancer to write the story.

Making Assignments: What to Say and How to Say It

When the editor is ready to assign to a freelancer a piece originated by the magazine, the next step is to telephone him. Contacting the freelancer by phone, rather than by mail or fax, is best because a phone conversation allows the freelancer to ask questions, and if he is not interested or is too busy to accept the assignment, the editor gets an immediate "no" and can then turn to her next choice to do the piece.

During the phone conversation the editor will describe the proposed piece to the freelancer, including (1) the angle or idea of the piece, (2) what the piece is expected to cover, (3) the tone of the piece (if it is to be light or humorous or critical, for example) and (4) the length of the piece, ordinarily expressed in the number of words. And if there is anything else the freelancer needs to know in order to understand what the assignment will require of him (acquisition of photos or hiring of a translator, for example), the editor will tell him that also.

If the freelancer wants to do the piece as described (some freelancers are picky about the subjects they write about and will turn down articles that fail to interest them), the editor will then give the freelancer a deadline for delivery. The editor weighs three considerations in specifying a deadline: (1) when the magazine absolutely must have the piece; (2) a reasonable amount of time necessary to report and write the piece; and (3) the natural tendency of many freelancers to miss their deadlines. Most articles can be done in about three weeks. Many require less time. Most writers, however, have a tendency to take as much time as you give them, often *more* than you give them, and they usually can do as well in three weeks as they will in six.

Here's a good way to present the deadline to the freelancer: "I need the piece in three weeks. Is that a problem?" If he answers, "No," he's agreeing to a three-week deadline. If he answers, "Yes," let him explain the problem and if you still want him to do the piece, extend the deadline. Of course, some articles, particularly investigative pieces, require more than three weeks, and in such cases the editor sets a realistic deadline or works one out with the freelancer.

In any event, always set a definite deadline. Always make it reasonably short, even when you don't plan to run the piece within the next ten months. Never tell a writer you need the piece "as soon as possible." For some writers, "as soon as possible" could be a year from next St. Urho's Day.

Even though he agrees to the three-week deadline, the freelancer may not make it. In fact, the wise editor assumes the freelancer will not make the deadline. In making assignments, the wise editor will have in his or her head *two* deadlines: One is the deadline given to the writer; the other is what Wesley Price, a former editor on *The Saturday Evening Post* and *Ladies' Home Journal*, called the "drop-dead deadline." That's the deadline by which the magazine absolutely must have the piece in hand if it is going to be published in a certain issue. The wise editor never lets the freelancer know what the drop-dead deadline is. The editor should give the freelancer a deadline that is, ideally, weeks in advance of the drop-dead deadline, so when the freelancer misses his deadline, the editor still has ample time to receive the piece, edit it and meet the production schedule for the issue in which the piece has been earmarked. If given the drop-dead deadline, the freelancer likely will take the additional time that it allows, and the editor and his staff will rush like mad to get the piece into the issue or pay additional production costs to crash the piece into the issue—or miss the issue altogether if the piece is even just a couple of days late. When making assignments, always remember to give yourself and your magazine the advantage.

After describing the piece and giving the freelancer a deadline, the editor will tell him what the fee will be. Fees are usually standard, all freelancers getting paid the same amount for pieces that are the same length. However, some magazines pay graduated fees, especially to freelancers who generate their own ideas for articles. A freelancer will get, say, $500 for the first piece he sells or writes for the magazine; he will get, say, $750 for the second piece and will get $1,000 for every piece after the second one. The idea behind the graduated fee is to reward proven performers and encourage them to keep submitting good ideas and good material to your magazine, instead of some other magazine.

Payment of the fee should be upon acceptance of the piece described by the editor and agreed to by the writer. Some magazines pay on publication, which is a cheap—in every sense of the word—way of doing business and one that's not to be recommended for reputable publications. If the freelancer is doing his first piece for your magazine, he needs to be told that your magazine pays on acceptance.

Reputable magazines also reimburse the freelancer for reasonable expenses incurred in reporting the piece. When telling the freelancer that the magazine will reimburse him for reasonable expenses, make sure to use the key word "reasonable." Flying first class is not a reasonable expense. If the freelancer has to rent a car, it can be a Ford Focus or even a Taurus. That's reasonable. A Lincoln is not reasonable. An ordinary single room in a motel or hotel is reasonable; a presidential suite is not. Furthermore, all expenses must be documented, so the freelancer should be advised to get receipts for everything. Advise him in a nice, casual way, however, and avoid sounding as if you don't trust him.

Reputable magazines pay kill fees, too. One way to tell the freelancer that your magazine will pay him a kill fee is to say, "And if for some reason the piece doesn't work out, we'll pay you a guarantee." It's not necessary to say what the guarantee, or kill fee, will be unless the freelancer asks. It shouldn't be so big that a freelancer is rewarded for handing in a piece of garbage, but it should be big enough so he doesn't feel he is going to take a complete bath if the piece flops. It probably ought to be 10 to 25 percent of the fee the freelancer would have received if the piece had been acceptable.

If the freelancer still wants to do the piece after hearing the financial arrangements, the next thing to say is that you will send him a letter confirming the assignment and the arrangements. It's a good idea to say also, "And in the letter I'll give you a little outline, so you can see how we think the piece might go." The idea is not to bind the writer to your concept of the piece, disallowing the use of his own judgment, but instead it is to let him know the essentials of the piece, so he can see the scope and coverage and even the possible organization of it. That letter, which the editor should write and send, by mail, fax or e-mail, immediately after the phone conversation, becomes a sort of contract between the magazine and the freelancer. It spells out the terms and it defines the piece. It is that piece, the one defined in the letter, that the magazine is ordering from the freelancer and for which it will pay the stated fee upon acceptance. If the writer fails to deliver *that* piece—he either delivers no piece at all or one that does not meet the description given by the editor on the telephone and outlined in the letter—the magazine is not obligated to pay the freelancer anything.

In the letter the editor will also tell the freelancer to let her know if he runs into serious problems—problems that could delay the piece or change the angle or, worst of all, kill the whole idea. All sorts of things can go wrong with an article, and the writer needs to notify his editor as soon as they do.

A friendly, upbeat sentence is a good way to end the letter. Something like, "Thanks for agreeing to take on the assignment, Dave (or whatever his or her name is), and we look forward to seeing the piece in three weeks."

The editor should keep track of the deadline for every piece assigned and when a deadline passes without the piece coming in, he should phone the writer to find out the status of the piece. As an assigning editor on four different magazines, I found it hard to make dunning phone calls. I'd keep hoping the piece would come in the next day. "It'll probably get here tomorrow," I'd tell myself, "and if it doesn't, then I'll call him." The next day I'd find myself saying the same thing. Sometimes the piece did arrive within a day or two of the deadline. Often, however, I eventually had to make the call. "Hi, Dave. How's the piece coming?" I'd ask. That one question ordinarily is enough to let the editor learn how close to completion the piece is and when she can expect it. Sometimes it takes another question: "So when can you get it to me, Dave?" If you have to ask that one, the piece is probably in trouble and the writer's answer will tell you how much trouble. But make sure you get a delivery date. Make him promise to give it to you by then.

Some pieces you'll never get, even though the freelancer keeps promising. It's a mystery why a writer would take on an assignment knowing he or she is not going to do it, but it happens.

Happily, such experiences with freelancers are rare. Many of them will deliver the piece on or before the deadline, and most within a few days of the deadline.

When a freelancer is given an assignment as a result of his or her query, the editor may make the assignment either by letter or phone (preferably by phone), and the piece the editor orders is ordinarily the one the freelancer proposed in the query, so there is little need for the editor to describe the piece to the freelancer. Aside from that one difference, an assignment to a querying freelancer follows the same procedure as an assignment for a piece the magazine originates. If the editor wants the freelancer to write the proposed piece with a different angle, of course, the editor will spell it out for the freelancer on the telephone and in the letter that follows.

When an article is assigned to a staff member, the editor should make sure the staffer understands what the editor wants. It's best to describe the piece to the staffer in the same way he would to a freelancer, even offering a suggested outline. Staffers going on an assignment should be reminded, too, about *reasonable* expenses and the need for receipts.

How to Get Good Content without Spending a Fortune

Good editorial content depends on good ideas, since poor ideas seldom result in anything but poor pieces. But good material does not require a big editorial budget. The editor who is enterprising and imaginative can bring quality content to the magazine almost regardless of the editorial budget. Here are some ways to acquire good material with limited resources:

■ *Pick unknown writers.* Writers who have already made a name for themselves among magazine editors are more likely to require a fee that a low-budget magazine can't pay. Don't covet what you can't have. Work with what you can afford. After all, *any* magazine editor can get good material if she's got a sky's-the-limit budget and can pay the going rate of well-known, sure-fire, high-performance authors. The test of a truly talented editor is finding good writers whom the world has not yet discovered and who therefore are much more likely to do good work cheap until the world does discover them.

Can such writers be found? Lester Markel, the late, legendary Sunday editor of *The New York Times* whose domain included *The New York Times Magazine*, the book review and the travel section, all of which used freelance authors, once asked a job applicant if he wanted to be a writer or an editor and when the young man said, "An editor," Markel told him, "That's good. Writers are a dime a dozen." A little blunt, as Markel often was, but nevertheless true, then and now. The magazine editor should realize it's a buyer's market in writers. Out there in America sits an abundant supply of capable writers—not Tom Wolfes, not Barbara Goldsmiths, but good enough to produce quality material if given the benefit of strong editing (which is something else the magazine editor is paid to do).

One of the best places to look for unknowns is other magazines: city magazines; regional magazines (such as *Down East*, *Arizona Highways*, *Chesapeake Bay Magazine*, *Adirondack Life*); small, special-interest magazines (such as *AAA Going Places*, *Salt Water Sportsman*, *Golden Years*, *Bird Watcher's Digest*); trade magazines that run profiles and other nontechnical pieces; newspapers' Sunday magazines. Also look in newspapers themselves, especially those that run a lot of local features.

To judge a writer's reporting and writing abilities, in order to decide if he or she can produce a quality piece for your magazine, look for anecdotes, descriptive detail, lively quotes, crisp narrative, specifics of all kinds. If a writer can deliver those elements, no matter the piece's structural faults, he can probably produce an eventually good, solid, readable piece for your magazine. Don't expect a perfect piece from the author's hands. Close is good enough. Settle for something that has the makings of a good piece (as listed above), something that can be edited or rewritten into a piece with a clear angle, effective lead, logical organization, appropriate conclusion and whatever else the original version lacks.

■ *Use experts.* Ordinarily, experts (scientists, physicians, lawyers, economists, historians, scholars, critics, technical specialists, authorities of every kind) make poor writers. But they *are* the experts—the sources your writer would use if you were paying a writer to do the article—*and* they often work cheap as writers. Scholars and other academicians especially do not write to be paid fees, but to be published. Many other experts are more interested in having their say and exerting an influence than they are in getting paid for what they write.

What's more, there are some experts who *can* write, who don't have to have heavy editing to make their pieces readable. *National Geographic* seems to do all right using experts. So do many other magazines. *Harvard Magazine*, Harvard University's outstanding alumni publication, does especially well using experts, many of whom are the university's faculty, administrators or alumni.

■ *Use eyewitnesses and participants.* It's not always necessary to have a *writer* cover a story. Sometimes a participant or an eyewitness can produce an editable story that will work nearly as well. For example, one of the runners entered in the Boston marathon might agree to write a piece about it. Someone going to Spain as a tourist might be persuaded to put Pamplona on her itinerary and take in the running of the bulls, then do an article on her experience. In such cases, arrangements with the person who will write the piece need to be made in advance of the event. It's important that the writer know beforehand that he is going to write an article about it and that he be coached by an editor on what to look for and what to include in the piece. Otherwise, there's a danger that the magazine will get not the piece you intended, but instead will get a "how I spent my summer vacation" story, full of cuteness, vagueness and unsupported generalizations.

It *is* possible to get an editable after-the-fact piece by someone who didn't know beforehand that he would be writing about the event or experience. In some cases, it's the only way. An eyewitness to a presidential assassination, for example, or the survivor of a shark attack might tell his story with such powerful narrative that the writing defects are virtually unnoticeable, or if they are noticeable, they merely add authenticity and credibility to the account. If his story is strong enough, his memory clear enough, an eyewitness to or a participant in a dramatic event may give you an eminently publishable first-person piece.

■ *Use Q&A interviews.* The question-and-answer piece places no fewer demands on the writer as an interviewer, but it immensely simplifies the writing part of his job. Any staffer who can carry on an interesting conversation and can use a tape recorder should be able to do a Q&A. Instead of having to extrude words from his brain, usually the hardest part of writing, the Q&A writer puts down the words of his subject. The Q&A writer becomes more like an editor than a writer, deciding which words to leave in and which to take out.

A Q&A can't replace a profile, but it can work well for certain subjects. It works best when the subject is a celebrity or a name of some kind or if not readily recognizable by name, has a job or role that is well known.

Preparation is the big key to Q&A success. The interviewer should know what to ask and talk about before going to the interview and should take along a list of topics to be covered. When the interview is over, the interviewer transcribes the tape, edits the transcript, then writes an editable or rewritable lead to go on top of the Q&A material and turns the piece over to the editor.

■ *Develop your staff.* A limited budget usually means limited salaries for editorial staff members, one consequence of which is that staff members are likely to be young and/or relatively inexperienced. Some of them, however, may be capable of becoming consistently good writers and producing quality material. Don't force them to develop on their own, to learn only by trial and error. Don't let them remain unaware of their reporting failures and writing faults. Take time to point out, in an instructive way, defects and deficiencies in staff-written pieces and give staffers a chance to correct them. Resist the temptation to fix it yourself because doing it yourself is quicker and easier than having to explain what you want. The editor's job includes the growing of staff members. Developing dependable writers among staffers who are already on the payroll can save freelance money for the times when you really need it.

■ *Use local writers.* If the story is in, say, Kansas City and the magazine is in, say, Atlanta, the editor can save a bundle in expense money by assigning the piece to a freelancer who is already in or near Kansas City, instead of flying a writer in, hiring a rental car, putting the writer up in a motel and buying meals for her. Look in newspapers, city magazines and other magazines in the area to discover possible authors if you don't already know one. To discover the names and addresses of magazines published in a particular city, look in one of the periodical directories available at a public library—Gale's, Ulrich's or Standard Rate and Data Service.

■ *Use previously published material.* Here is one of the best ways to get first-class content at economy-class prices. The editor needs to be forever on the lookout for not only story ideas but for material published in other magazines, in newspapers and in books. Read an assortment of magazines to find which ones run pieces suitable for your magazine's audience. Use *Reader's Guide to Periodical Literature*, *The New York Times Index* and the Nexus data bank to locate or browse for articles and features appropriate for your magazine. Read *Publisher's Weekly*, the trade magazine of the book publishing industry, to keep up with new books in your magazine audience's subject area. To find books already published, use *Subject Guide to Books in Print* and library data banks. You can also use the websites of online booksellers to search for books by subject. Barnes & Noble (www.bn.com), for example, lists virtually every book in print in English and many that are out of print.

Unless the magazine that originally published the piece has a large, general circulation, such as *Time*, *Newsweek* or *Reader's Digest*, chances are small that your magazine's readers will have already read the piece, and for most of your readers it will be new.

Ordinarily, all that is necessary is to make a written request for permission to reprint from a newspaper or magazine. Sometimes the original publication will require a reprint fee, usually based on the circulation and nature of your magazine. It's not necessary to buy any sort of rights to the piece; merely ask for permission to reprint. In some cases the article's author will hold the copyright to the piece, and the original publication will pass your request for permission along to him or his agent. In such cases, the fee may be substantially larger than the publication would ask. Don't be shy about negotiating the fee—and don't pay more than a token fee unless it's a piece you think your magazine's readers absolutely must have. (It might be useful for you to know that some magazines also permit reuse of their photographs.)

Book publishers generally are more accustomed to receiving and granting requests for permission to use their material than are newspapers and magazines. Book publishers operate on the premise that book excerpts help book sales and therefore book publishers are usually agreeable to a request for permission to excerpt. When you make the request, specify how many words you want to use and on which pages in the book they appear. Book publishers are more likely to grant permission when the proposed excerpt constitutes only a small percentage of the book's content.

The best way to excerpt is to find a chapter that presents one central idea, like an angle in a magazine article, or one episode in the case of fiction or narrative nonfiction. Find a chapter that more or less stands on its own, so that characters or background or other vitally connected material does not have to be captured from preceding or following chapters. Occasionally, however, some background, explanation or other introductory material will have to be removed from an earlier chapter or two and woven into the first part of the excerpted chapter. The publisher should be told if you intend to use even slightly more than the chapter you are asking to excerpt.

In addition to providing quality content for your magazine, book excerpts are often highly promotable, giving the editor—and the circulation department—an opportunity to call readers' attention to the issue in which it appears and to the magazine in general.

In the same way that book publishers believe excerpts *help* book sales, they tend to think condensations *hurt* sales. Therefore, condensations are likely to cost more than you want your magazine to pay.

■ *Hold a writing contest.* Contests for amateur writers or ordinary readers of your magazine can yield a surprising number of usable pieces, particularly first-person, personal-experience stories. Many magazines have had good results with contests. Over the years, *Guideposts* magazine, which specializes in first-person stories, has had outstandingly good results running writing contests for high school students. Its methods may be worth following. It announces the contest and presents the rules in one or more issues of the magazine, promotes the issue in which names of the winners will appear, announces the winners and publishes the top winner in that issue, and publishes other winners' pieces in later issues. Winning stories become the property of the magazine.

Guideposts awards the top winners college scholarships, which together amount to a considerable sum. But the top cash prize for a winning story probably need not be more than your magazine would ordinarily pay for an article, and winners other than the first-place winner can be awarded smaller amounts for pieces that are perhaps just as usable as the No. 1 winner's.

CHAPTER 6

The Editorial Process

W hen manuscripts, from freelancers or staff members, are received in the editorial department, they begin a journey through the editorial process, to be read, evaluated, decided on and acted on in one or more ways. The editor will adopt or adapt the processing system already in place at an established magazine or, if the magazine is a start-up, will devise a system that works best for him or her in the new situation. The main idea is to create an orderly process for handling all pieces that come to or originate in the editorial offices, some of which will find their way into the magazine and many that won't.

Keeping Track of the Material

The wise editor will want some way to quickly learn the status of every assigned piece, especially pieces that have been tentatively scheduled into an issue or in which the editor is for other reasons particularly interested. And so some system for keeping track of every assigned piece is needed.

The best system is one that creates an entry as soon as a piece is assigned, either to a freelancer or staffer. The entry will include the author's name, the working title of the piece, the date assigned, the due date, perhaps the intended length of the piece, the piece's current status and the name of the assigning editor. Other information, such as illustration possibilities, might also be included. The entries usually will be filed alphabetically by authors' last names. If the entries are computerized—and what today isn't?—it is easy enough for the editor to find the piece he wants by doing a word search in the working titles if he can't remember the author's name. The working title should be concise, but should contain the main idea of the piece, to jog the editor's memory of the piece and to aid a word search.

As assigned pieces are received, the entries are updated to show that the pieces are in-house and to tell briefly where they are and what's happening to them—their current status, in other words. Once the pieces have been accepted for publication, the entries can be transferred to the inventory, providing the editor with a list of all the pieces that are on hand and available for scheduling into the magazine. Unsolicited pieces that have been accepted will also be listed in the inventory, which can be printed out and given to concerned staff members prior to scheduling meetings.

How to Evaluate the Material

When assigned pieces come to the magazine, they need to be read and have a decision made on their acceptability. On a magazine with a very small staff, the editor may do all the reading and all the decision-making alone. Most editors, however, will probably want to share the load.

The Article Evaluation Form

One way for the editor to share the load is to have the assigning editor read the piece first, then fill out an article evaluation form. The form, which can be created on a computer, would call for the name of the author, name of the assigning editor, date received in the editorial office, a working title for the piece, a summary of the piece and the evaluation itself. The assigning editor would attach the completed form to the manuscript—or, better yet, to a photocopy of the manuscript, to guard against its possible loss—and then pass the piece plus evaluation form to another editor for his or her reading and evaluation, using the same form.

The editor ultimately decides on the piece, but does so with the advantage of having other staffers' opinions and suggestions, which will be detailed on the evaluation form, with each reading editor making comments and signing his or her name to the comments. Such a set of reading and evaluating editors is often called a *reading line*. The editor decides who is on it and perhaps prescribes the order in which the reading-line editors read the pieces.

Completely computerized magazines may have authors submit their pieces either via modem or on floppy disks, and the pieces will be input by the assigning editors into the magazine's network as computer files. Assigning editors in those cases, of course, will use a computerized version of the article evaluation form and input their comments and suggestions to accompany the files, which can then be called up on the screens of the editor and other reading-line editors.

Unsolicited Pieces

Unsolicited pieces from known authors, writers who have written for the magazine before or who are otherwise known to an editor, ordinarily will come addressed to a particular editor and will enter the editorial process through the editor who receives the manuscript.

Other unsolicited pieces that have potential for publication may be handled in a similar way. The first editor who reads an unsolicited piece that he or she believes might be usable will fill out an evaluation form and pass the manuscript and the attached form to another editor or to *the* editor, following whatever procedure the editor decides works best.

Magazines that don't consider unsolicited material from unknown authors are likely to simply drop it into the wastepaper basket. Or if a self-addressed, stamped envelope is included with the manuscript, the piece may be returned with a form rejection note saying, more or less, "Thanks for sending this to us, but we are unable to consider unsolicited material now."

What to Look For

In evaluating an article—and, usually, smaller pieces as well—the editor, and all other editors on the reading line, will read it carefully, sometimes more than once, to see what's in it and what's not. After reading it, editors should ask themselves the following seven questions. Does the piece have:

1. A clear angle? The piece must be about something—not *all about* something, but something about something. If it's a profile, for example, it should not be a biography; it should be about some part or aspect of the subject's life. Other material may be included, but the piece should focus on something specific. The piece should convey a main message, a central idea or major theme. It should not be merely a fact sheet or encyclopedia entry. It ought to make one big, overriding point—but not more than one. More than one angle is no angle.

Furthermore, if it's an assigned piece, the angle should be the same one described to the author when the piece was assigned.

2. An effective lead? A lead is supposed to (a) stop the perusing reader, (b) introduce the subject and (c) draw the reader into the piece. What's more, the lead should not merely introduce the subject, but should introduce it within the context of the angle. For example, if the piece is about the first lady being her husband's most enthusiastic campaigner, the lead should show her in connection with a campaign, not in her kitchen or selecting new draperies.

The editor must decide if the author's lead does what a lead is supposed to do.

3. A clear justifier? The justifier—or peg—is a sentence or paragraph, maybe more than one paragraph, that (a) tells the reader what's going on in the lead if it isn't obvious, (b) tries to establish newsworthiness, or relevance, in order to give the reader a reason to read the piece and (c) hints at what is to come and what the reader will find out by reading the piece. The justifier is the link between the lead and the body of the piece.

4. Anecdotes and other narrative? The piece, whatever its subject or angle, must be readable—interesting and easy to read—and the most effective way to make it readable is to use anecdotes and/or other narrative. The piece should have anecdotes that illustrate, that support generalizations, that *show* the subject to the reader. Narrative is the kind of writing that shows action, unlike exposition, which merely explains or tells. The piece ought to show, not just tell.

5. Lively quotes, descriptive detail and other specifics? A piece needs, as William Emerson, a former editor of *The Saturday Evening Post*, used to say, voices. It should let the reader hear someone other than the author.

The piece should also let the reader see—and hear and smell and feel—for himself. Insofar as possible, the piece ought to always be showing the reader something, making pictures form in the reader's mind, because pictures, particularly action pictures, are much more interesting and much more likely to hold the reader's interest than abstractions.

The piece should avoid vagueness and generalities by giving the reader specifics—names, dates, places, times, identifications, numbers, all the appropriate and needed details.

6. *A logical organization?* The material shouldn't be simply dumped onto the pages of the manuscript and left for the reader to sort out. It should be arranged and presented to the reader in a logical, make-sense, what-does-the-reader-need-to-know-next sequence.

7. *An appropriate conclusion?* The piece should not simply peter out or end abruptly. It should have a conclusion that lets the reader feel satisfied by the piece in the same way a diner, having eaten the dessert, feels satisfied by a meal.

The Repair and Salvage of Articles and Other Text

It's possible for a piece to be perfect as submitted by the author—possible, but not very likely. Almost every piece, no matter the author, the subject or the magazine for which it's written, will have something wrong with it.

And so after an editor reads the piece, notices its defects and reaches a judgment about it, which he or she will write on the article evaluation form, the next step is to figure out what should be done to fix it—or, in the case of a piece severely defective or deficient, how to salvage it. The opinions and suggestions of the reading-line editors will vary, of course, and *the* editor, with the advantage of other editors' ideas, will decide what is to be done with the piece.

Every editor should be mindful that an editor is supposed to be more than a voter—someone who turns thumbs up or thumbs down on a piece, pronouncing it good or bad, voting to accept or reject. An editor is also supposed to be more than a critic—someone who merely details a piece's faults and its author's failings.

Editors who are worth their salaries must say not only what's wrong with a piece but how to make the piece right. They must specify what they think should be done to fix it and make it publishable—like a physician who, after an examination and diagnosis, prescribes treatment to make the patient well.

It's just too easy for an editor to read a problematic piece and effortlessly blow it off. *The* editor, particularly when tired, impatient or frustrated, may also feel like throwing up his or her hands over a botched piece. But the editor, of all people, can't afford such an indulgence.

The editor's attitude should always be, "Let's save this piece if we possibly can." The guiding principle is: If the idea was good enough for us to assign the piece, it's good enough for us to try to save what the author has given us.

Besides trying to save the piece to rescue the idea, there is a matter of money. By now the magazine probably has expense money invested in the piece, and an honest effort should be made to protect the magazine's investment.

The editor should expect that let's-save-it-if-we-possibly-can attitude from the magazine's other editors. Editors whose article-evaluation comments are consistently negative need to be called into the editor's office and told that they can be a lot more help to the editor and to the magazine if they will suggest solutions instead of just pointing out problems.

Of course, not all troubled pieces can be saved. But killing a piece should always be the absolutely last resort. The editor should not pull the plug unless there is no hope whatever for resuscitation.

In most cases, however, a major revision is probably not necessary. What is usually necessary is merely some fixing, to make the piece as complete and readable as it can be within the limits of time, the available material and the author's ability.

Making the Revisions

Once the editor has decided what needs to be done to the piece, the next step is to describe the planned revision to the person who is going to make it.

Ordinarily it is best to have the author do the revision. Writers who take pride in their work will usually want to revise their own pieces, and the magazine probably owes it to them to let them handle the repairs. Besides that, the author is getting paid for the work, so why not let him do it? The assigning editor then, equipped with the editor's blueprint for revision, will tell the author, in writing or orally while the author takes notes, what more he needs to do to make the piece acceptable. The assigning editor also gives the author a deadline—a short one—for making the repairs and getting the piece back to the magazine.

When the revised piece is received, the assigning editor ordinarily will read it, complete a new article-evaluation form and send the revision and the new evaluation and perhaps the old evaluation and a copy of the letter that ordered the revision—all of the piece's barnacles—to the editor.

Sometimes the piece will need further work. If the additional work required is minor, the editor may ask a staff member to do it, or may have the piece sent back to the author with new instructions, particularly if time is not a problem.

If the further work is major, the editor must decide whether the piece is worth the additional effort to save it. If the answer is yes, the editor will probably want to turn the piece over to someone else. When the author of a botched piece also botches the rewrite, chances are that he or she simply isn't up to the assignment, and if the editor is going to get a usable piece out of the mess, someone else will have to write it.

The editor should have no reservations about turning the piece over to someone else. The author had his chance and struck out. The editor may then decide to pay the author the kill fee and reassign the piece to another freelancer. Or he might salvage some of the material, compensate the author for it and assign a new author to do whatever remains to be done with the piece, perhaps giving a shared byline to both authors or otherwise acknowledging the original author when the piece runs.

A cheaper and simpler solution would be to turn the piece over to a staff member, particularly if most of the trouble is in the writing rather than the reporting. On a small magazine, of course, the editor himself/herself would probably take over the piece.

If the original piece was assigned not to a freelancer but to a staffer, the editor would follow a similar procedure: Explain to the staffer what more needs to be done to the piece, give him a deadline, evaluate the revision and if the piece needs still more work, have the writer try again. If a lot of work is required and the editor is eager for the piece and the deadline is rapidly approaching, then the editor can turn the piece over to another staffer or, on a small magazine, do the additional rewrite himself/herself.

Acceptance or Rejection

Eventually the editor decides to accept or reject the piece. If the piece is rejected, the author is notified (usually by the assigning editor and probably in a letter, since bad news is easier to deliver by mail than in person or over the phone), a check is requisitioned for the author's kill fee and documented expenses, and the piece is removed from the list of pieces in the works.

If the piece is accepted, the author is notified (usually by the assigning editor and sometimes by phone, since good news is more happily delivered voice-to-voice than through the mail), a check is requisitioned for payment and documented expenses, the piece's entry in the list of pieces in the works is updated and transferred to the magazine's active inventory and the piece itself is turned over to the magazine's copy editors or, in the case of a small magazine, is now ready to be copyread by the editor.

Copyediting

Depending on the size of the magazine, the tasks of copyediting may be borne by a single editor or by a battery of editors in a copy-editing department. On many magazines those who perform the copyediting tasks are called copy editors; on small magazines with bare-bones staffs, the editors who copyedit are likely to be more than just copy editors.

Whatever the size of the magazine, however, someone has to do the copyediting, for although it can seem one of the least glamorous jobs in the editorial department, it is certainly one of the most important. Copy editors, or whoever does what they do, are the editorial department's last line of defense against mistakes in copy. Those mistakes can include anything from misspelled or misused words that make the magazine appear inept, to fact errors that misinform readers and embarrass the magazine, to potentially libelous statements that can injure the innocent and/or expose the magazine to costly and damaging litigation.

Ordinarily there are four main parts to the copyediting job: fact checking, language straightening, styling and trimming.

Fact Checking

Many big magazines, with large staffs and ample resources, devote considerable time, money and peoplepower to fact-checking, to make sure that authors have their facts straight and that mistakes of any kind do not get into print. Some magazines have extensive libraries that their copy editors use to verify information in pieces they plan to publish. If their own reference materials are unable to provide verification, copy editors will telephone public libraries or other sources to seek verification.

Everything that looks like a fact in a manuscript, including all proper nouns, will be checked and when it is verified, will perhaps be marked on the manuscript so that the editor will know the information has been verified. If the information cannot be verified or if the copy editor's research discovers information at odds with the author's, the copy editor may telephone the author to resolve whatever seems problematic.

In such cases, if the author's source seems more authoritative than the copy editor's, the author's information will usually stand. If the copy editor's source seems more authoritative, the piece may be edited to include the more authoritative version or, in some cases, the disputed information may simply be deleted. When the disputed information is important to the story, the editor should decide what is to be done with it, since editors who are purely copy editors ordinarily don't have authority to make big decisions.

On magazines that are not large the same need to check facts exists. All pieces entering the magazine's inventory should, as part of the copy-editing process, be routinely and carefully checked for factual accuracy. The editor should build enough time into the magazine's production schedule to allow careful fact-checking in cases where pieces are accepted and immediately scheduled into the next issue.

The editor should see that the magazine's copy editor, or the editor who performs as such, is equipped with at least some basic reference works, including a dictionary (the biggest and newest possible), a current almanac, *Facts on File*, *The New York Times Index*, a road atlas, a gazetteer, *Who's Who in America*, Bartlett's or some other good book of quotations, a set of encyclopedias if possible, *The New York Times Guide to Reference Materials* and, in the case of special-interest magazines, directories of people, companies, organizations and agencies connected with that special interest.

Many of those reference works are now available as computer databases, and those that aren't probably soon will be. In the meantime, the magazine's copy editor can use the printed references to check facts.

Facts on File and *The New York Times Index*, of course, may be used not only to verify dates, names, places and a few other bare facts but can also be used by the copy editor to lead him or her to appropriate issues of *The New York Times* or a local newspaper on microfilm to check additional facts.

Language Straightening

Good copy editors let nothing in the author's words escape their critical eyes. They catch and correct grammatical errors and misspelled or misused words; they resolve ambiguities (with the author's help if necessary) and remove them; they rewrite awkward or unclear phrases into smooth, understandable prose. They are the finishers and polishers of the magazine's content.

Styling

Every publication needs a policy to govern the use of abbreviations, numerals, capitalization, punctuation, names, courtesy titles, spelling preferences, obscenity, slang, etc. and, in some cases, how certain parts of the copy will be set in type. That policy, or those policies, of the publication is called its style. The publication's style gives the publication consistency and avoids forcing editors to either accept the author's style (or, more likely, the author's lack of style) or having to redecide each time the occasion arises whether, for example, it's Pennsylvania Avenue or Pennsylvania Ave.

A magazine may adopt the style of another publication or publisher, or it may devise its own, usually by borrowing from several different styles. Ideally the style is set forth in a *stylebook*, which is a collection, sometimes printed and bound, of all the specifics of the style.

Magazines generally tend to use a style that is more like book styles than newspaper or wire-service styles. One major concern of newspapers and wire services is space, and so their styles tend to shorten text a bit through use of abbreviations, numerals, last names only after the first reference, and so on. Book and magazine styles, on the other hand, tend to spell things out and take more space, because doing so looks better to the eye of the reader and sounds better to his mind's ear.

Copy editors are supposed to be the ultimate authority on all matters of style and they are to faithfully apply the magazine's style to all content.

Trimming

Copy editors also are ordinarily entrusted with the task of trimming pieces to their optimum length or to the size of the space into which they are to fit in the magazine.

There's a difference between trimming and cutting. Cutting connotes deleting parts of the story, taking out sizable chunks, either for space reasons or because the material is irrelevant or of questionable authenticity or possibly libelous or something else that has nothing to do with space. Copy editors ordinarily don't make such cuts—unless they're given specific instructions by the editor or someone the editor delegates to instruct the copy editor. But copy editors do trim, snipping out a little bit here, a little bit there to reduce the number of lines in the piece.

The Final Stage

When a manuscript (or a computer document) has been copyedited, it has reached the end of the editorial process and, upon being scheduled into an issue, is ready to begin a new phase as it makes its way into the magazine.

CHAPTER 7

Planning an Issue

With a full inventory of content on hand, the editor is ready to build an issue. As is the case with anything else being constructed, the way to make a magazine is to plan first, build second.

The editor usually will have some particular pieces in mind for a particular issue, but he or she will want to involve other key members of the staff in planning an issue, to get their views and suggestions and arrive at what the editor hopes will be a consensus on the issue's content.

The usual way to do so is to hold scheduled issue-planning meetings, where issues first begin to take shape.

The Planning Meeting

One good way to conduct issue-planning meetings is to provide the editors who attend—plus the art director, who also attends—with a copy of the inventory list in advance of the meeting, to allow them time to study the list and come prepared to offer suggestions about which pieces might be scheduled.

Those who attend are also provided with an issue dummy, which is a diagram of the issue, showing all the pages of the issue, including covers, arranged as spreads. If it's a commercial magazine, running advertising, the dummy will probably come from the advertising department. If it's a large commercial magazine, the dummy may come from a special department, perhaps called the scheduling department. The dummy will show which ads go on which pages and will also show which pages and which columns on certain pages are for editorial use.

If the magazine is not a commercial magazine or does not run advertising for some other reason, the editor (or someone he or she designates) will provide the dummy, showing all blank pages, since there are no ads.

As pieces are scheduled, perhaps only tentatively at first and subject to considerable mind-changing later, the staff members write the pieces' working titles onto the dummy to show which pages the pieces will occupy in the issue. The dummy will also show where the ads go, so that when the dummy is completed, the editor and the magazine's staff will be able to see, almost at a glance, where everything in the issue goes and what is on each page of the issue.

Some magazines, either in addition to or instead of using issue dummies, will use tiles—on some magazines they're about the size and shape of Formica samples—to represent the pages of an issue and will hang the tiles on a wall of the staff conference room, using hooks that allow the tiles to be taken down, altered, moved around and put back up. Working titles are written on the tiles with an erasable marker. That system allows the editor and other concerned staffers to see the sweep of the entire issue and to make changes easily by shifting the tiles to new positions, indicating a piece's move to other pages.

The editor, of course, is the planning meeting's leader and comes prepared with his or her choices for the issue. All pieces suggested for the issue, by the editor and by the other staffers, are discussed before decisions are made about which pieces are going into the issue.

Establishing the Right Editorial Mix

The editor normally lives in dread of a day when there's not enough material to make an issue. The prudent editor, therefore, will want enough pieces in the inventory at all times to make three or more issues. With that much material on hand, the editor will be assured of not only sufficient quantity but, usually, of sufficient variety.

Each issue of the magazine needs a variety of content. With some magazines, the variety, or editorial mix, is the same in nearly every issue. Every issue, let's say, would need: a cover story, which would be a serious, multi-source, reporting piece of 3,500 words or more; a profile; a light piece; a how-to piece; the magazine's usual standing features; some shorts; and either a photo feature or an article that is photo-intensive. Each issue would contain at least those pieces.

In that case, the editor may not want *two* big, serious pieces, one the cover story and one elsewhere. The editor probably doesn't want more than one how-to piece or more than one profile or more than one photo feature in the same issue.

A magazine's editorial mix might require not different *kinds* of pieces, but pieces on different subjects, perhaps the same assortment of subjects every issue. For an example, look at the pieces in *Time*. Typically there are in each issue pieces about significant events, people and developments in the United States, national stories; there are also pieces about significant events, people and developments outside the United States, international stories; and there are pieces about business, science, culture, entertainment and sports; plus the magazine's standing features, such as People.

The editorial mix is an important part of a magazine's personality and identity. It may be the big reason the subscriber subscribes and the newsstand buyer buys. When planning each issue, the magazine's editor, and the other staff members as well, must consider the editorial mix, making sure that all or most of the appropriate ingredients are included.

Scheduling the Book

Deciding which pieces will go into an issue and where in the issue they will go is called, on many magazines, scheduling the book, and it is the main thing that happens at issue planning meetings.

There is often among editors a tendency to put into the magazine the best pieces they've seen lately. The wise editor will recognize that tendency in herself and judiciously resist it. Repeatedly yielding to it is likely to result in an inventory grown stale, as older pieces again and again take a back seat to the newest material.

On the other hand, there is a valid argument for scheduling into the current issue the very best pieces in the inventory. The argument is founded on the same let's-put-our-best-athletes-on-the-field principle that coaches use to assure their best chance of winning. Editors need to realize, though, that if they run their ten or twelve best pieces in the current issue, by the next issue they'll have to come up with another ten or twelve best pieces or face an inventory of second-bests and worse. The feast-or-famine result will likely be a sensational issue followed by a weak-tea issue.

A good procedure to use in scheduling the book is to first schedule the pieces that must be included in the issue, because of timeliness, urgency or seasonality or because they are standard ingredients in the editorial mix. The standard ingredients—in any magazine's editorial mix—will always include a cover story, which should be a piece worthy of being a cover story (see Chapter 14 for help in picking a cover piece).

After all the "must" pieces have been pencilled in on the issue dummy, then the editor and the other staffers planning the issue can consider pieces for the remaining pages.

Some of the considerations to be applied in selecting the remaining pieces—and in choosing between competing "must" pieces:

■ *Variety of subjects.* Make the issue offer an array of subjects. Don't repeat or overlap subjects unless you have a good reason.

■ *Variety of lengths.* The goal is give the reader not all long pieces, not all short pieces, not all medium-length pieces—and to pace the issue so that long pieces are not immediately followed by another long piece, short pieces are not immediately followed by other short pieces.

■ *Variety of tone.* Avoid having too many heavy pieces, too many light pieces, too many pieces that sound the same.

■ *Variety of openers.* Make sure some pieces open on a single page, some on a spread; avoid too many consecutive spread openers and too many consecutive single-page openers.

■ *Use of photographs.* A magazine is supposed to be a visual medium; make sure you schedule some pieces that lend themselves to illustration with attractive, interesting photos—not merely photos, but photos that attract and hold the reader's interest.

■ *Promotability.* The cover story naturally should be one that will be promotable on the cover and help sell the magazine on the newsstand and help drive the subscriber inside the magazine to read it. But the cover piece shouldn't be expected or required to carry the whole load. Each issue should contain several pieces for which cover lines can be written to promote the issue by promoting those particular pieces of content.

■ *The center spread.* This is one of the commandments of issue planning: Remember the center spread to keep it special. In saddle-stitched magazines the center spread is the only spread where a photograph or artwork illustration spanning the entire spread can be reproduced without having to jump the gutter and run the risk of colors not matching across the gutter or the illustration or type not being aligned across the gutter.

Therefore the editor and the art director should take advantage of the center spread's opportunity to print from one side of the spread to the other, uninterrupted by the gutter. Many magazines sell the center spread to advertisers—at a premium price—and so it is lost to editorial content. But when the center spread is available for editorial content, the issue should be scheduled to use the center spread for something special, something with visual impact.

■ *Competing displays.* The issue should be scheduled so the display of one piece does not compete with the display of another piece for the reader's attention. For example, if an article opens on a right-hand page, with a big photo, title, subtitle and other display elements, that right-hand page should not face a one-pager, with its own display elements, on the other side of the spread. One-page openers and one-pagers should face an ad or the final page of text of the article that precedes it in the issue.

Where's the Color?

Not all magazines enjoy the unlimited use of four-color process, or even spot color. On many magazines, particularly the small ones, four-color is restricted to certain signatures because the expense of printing four-color on every signature is more than the magazine can afford.

So one other huge consideration in planning an issue is: Where's the color? The magazine's advertising department, or the scheduling department, has the answer, because they know which ads are four-color, which pages the color ads are scheduled on and therefore which signatures are going to be printed with four-color process.

If the magazine does not depend on advertising for four-color but is limited in its use because of the expense, the printer can always tell the editor which pages are included in which signatures.

For example, if a 64-page magazine is limited to one 16-page, four-color signature and the cover must be four-color, the editor needs to know which pages are in the same signature as the cover. Or if the magazine can afford two 16-page, four-color signatures, the editor needs to know which pages go in which signature so he or she can choose the one that best accommodates the illustration in the issue.

When an issue is being planned, then, pieces with four-color illustration will be scheduled onto the pages that have four-color available. On pages that do not have four-color available (unless the magazine pays extra to have four-color on them) the editor and the other key staffers will schedule only pieces that will be illustrated with black-and-white photographs or artwork.

End-to-End Makeup or Jumps?

It's a question of design, but it affects the planning of the issue. Some magazines open some of their articles with display and some text, then jump the rest of the text to pages farther back in the book, in the same way a newspaper starts stories on page one, then jumps them to an inside page.

Other magazines, probably most, prefer end-to-end makeup, whereby every piece begins on a page or spread and continues on the following pages uninterrupted (except perhaps by advertising) until the piece ends.

It's a good guess that readers generally prefer end-to-end, so that one story ends before the next one begins and so they don't have to flip through pages to find the jump before they can continue reading. Jumps, to many readers, are an annoyance. And what editor wants to annoy readers?

Jumping *can* give the magazine a livelier look, however, especially issues with upwards of, say, 160 pages. Instead of having gray text appear throughout the book, magazines with jumps can move the grayness toward the back of the book, allowing the editor to place display-rich opening pages and spreads closer together to give the issue a busier look and faster pace at the front and middle of the book.

The Undulating Effect

If end-to-end makeup is the choice, the editor, in planning the issue, needs to carefully consider the sequence of the pieces of content. If an issue contains, say, twelve pieces, not all of the twelve will be equally strong and readable; one will be the strongest or best piece, and another will be twelfth best, with all others somewhere in between. The idea then is to avoid placing the six strongest pieces in the front of the book and the six weakest pieces in the back, the weakest of all being the last piece in the issue. When the pieces are arranged that way, the issue tends to taper off or peter out.

The desired effect is an undulating set of contents. Leading the issue would be a strong piece (not necessarily the cover story), then following it would be a piece that is less strong, then another strong piece, then something less strong, and so on throughout the issue. Something fairly strong should be reserved as the final piece in the issue, so that the strength of the content—along with reader interest—rises, instead of declining, at the issue's conclusion.

Heeding that same principle, magazines that use jumps and stack them toward the back of the book usually run a standing feature or fairly strong piece as the very last piece in the issue, providing an anchor for the issue.

Accommodating the Advertising

The editor, and the rest of the magazine's staff as well, should never lose sight of the importance of the magazine's advertisers. Commercial magazines owe their existence—and their payrolls—to advertising, so it's only reasonable that the advertisers who are footing the magazine's bills and the editors' salaries be given special consideration when it comes to placing their ads in an issue. Advertising is a fact of life, and the editor and the magazine's art director must learn to live with it.

In an ideal world, however, the magazine's publisher would create in each issue an editorial well, a set of pages reserved for editorial content only. Ads would be restricted to the front of the book and the back of the book, interspersed with some editorial material—letters to the editor, for example, and other short features. But the middle of the book would be strictly for the presentation of editorial content. And the editor could plan accordingly.

CHAPTER 8

Displaying the Content

T he successful editor realizes that his magazine's content is not merely published; it is *presented* to the reader. The pieces in an issue are like gifts, attractively packaged and wrapped to make them more compelling.

A helpful way to view the content is to see each piece in an issue as a worthwhile, desirable, perhaps even needed piece of reading material that the editor is calling to the reader's attention. The magazine then becomes like a department store, where interesting, useful, needed and delightful objects are displayed to their best advantage in settings that enhance their appeal and draw customers irresistibly to them. The objects are not stacked in boxes in a bleak storeroom; they are invitingly *displayed* in alluring settings. So, too, is a magazine's content.

The Elements of Display

The editor uses a variety of display elements to attract readers to the magazine's content. The elements include a piece's title and subtitle, the photographs and/or artwork that illustrate the piece, the captions that explain or identify the photos or illustrations, blurbs that emphasize parts of the story, typography (the artful use of type), computer-generated graphics, graphic devices (such as bars, bullets, borders, cap initials, etc.) and color.

The major, and probably crucial, elements of display, however, are those on a piece's opening page or spread, which is the page or pages in the magazine where the piece begins. It is there where readers are generally won or lost. The editor must make sure that each piece of content, on its opening page or spread, is displayed as well as it can be within the magazine's limits of money and time.

Kinds of Display

There are three basic ways to display a piece, and the editor, in concert with the magazine's art director, chooses the one most appropriate for the particular piece of content. When money or time is a tight restraint, the choice is made on the basis of feasibility as well as appropriateness.

In every case a piece will have a title, which is the most fundamental element of display. A piece ordinarily will also have a subtitle, a second display element. Those two elements are virtually indispensable, regardless of the nature or length of the piece, and of course they always appear on the opening page or spread. It is the elements *in addition to* the title and subtitle that provide the editor a choice.

On the opening page or spread of each piece of content, the editor may choose to display with photos, artwork illustrations, or with type only.

Display with Photographs

Despite everything that has altered values since the maxim was first uttered, a picture is still worth about a thousand words. Therefore, when you want to make a quick, dramatic statement to the reader, photographs are often the best way to do it. For the opening page or spread, *one* photo is usually all that's necessary. If more than one is needed, one of them should be dominant, in size and visual effect. Other photos can illustrate the piece on the pages following the opening page or spread.

Photographs have the advantage of authenticity. They say, "This is real." In many cases the editor will want a display that projects or certifies the authenticity of the article. If so, photographs are the appropriate display choice.

Display with Artwork Illustration

Photographs sometimes are not a possibility. Personal-experience stories often are about something that happened without having been recorded on film. For example, a Navy helicopter pilot is forced to land on an Antarctic ice floe during a storm, then manages to survive three days and nights without provisions or heat before being rescued. The story of his adventure could not be illustrated by photographs showing him during the time he spent on the ice. No such photos exist. To display that story the best way possible, the editor might decide to use artwork illustration—a painting that captures a dramatic moment of the pilot's experience.

An article about the days of the dinosaurs or a piece about the life of pre-Columbian American Indians (both of those stories ran in *National Geographic*) presents similar problems. In such cases, artwork illustration may be the best choice for display.

In other cases, photographs are *too* realistic. They do not capture the mood or the feeling evoked by a nostalgic piece, for example, or by a romantic or a lighthearted or humorous piece. In those cases, artwork illustration may display the piece best even though photographs are available.

Another reason to use artwork illustration is variety. The editor should be careful to avoid displaying every piece in an issue in the same way. The editor should strive for variety not only in content but in display.

Display with Type Only

Some pieces, because of the nature of their subjects, are best handled with a stark, bold, straightforward display. Placing photographs or artwork illustration on the opening page or spread of such a piece tends to weaken the message of the piece's title and subtitle. Here's an example:

WILL YOU BE THE NEXT
VICTIM OF DATE RAPE?
One of every four college women will be raped by an acquaintance before she graduates. Here's what you can do to avoid becoming a victim of the fastest growing crime in America.

To display that story effectively, the editor may choose to let the type of the title and subtitle be the only display elements on the opening page. If so, the typeface and point size selected for the title must be appropriate both for the piece and for the intended effect on the reader. A heavy, blunt face set in a large point size would probably work best.

Other kinds of pieces require other typefaces, of course. A nostalgic essay about grandmothers, for example, would need a typeface appropriate to the subject and tone of the piece.

Using only type to display a piece is especially appropriate for pieces that occupy less than a page in the magazine. Variety of display is another reason the editor may choose to use type only. Or when nothing else seems to work, type-only may be the editor's last resort.

Besides those three basic kinds of display, there is one other display choice the editor can make, of course, and that is a combination of photographs and artwork. In such cases, one will be the dominant element and one will be subordinate. The two disparate elements should not compete for the reader's attention.

Functions of the Display Elements

It's important for the editor to keep in mind the purposes of the display elements lest they tyrannize him. The display elements do not exist for their own sake, but primarily for the sake of the text and secondarily for the sake of the magazine as a whole. Photographs are not published in the magazine because by themselves they are great works of art. They are published because they are great—or at least adequate—photographs that *support the story*. The same goes for artwork illustrations and typography. The only exception is picture stories, where the natural order is reversed—the photos tell the story and are supported by text blocks and/or captions.

Understanding the functions of the display elements can help the editor keep photos, artwork, graphics, titles and blurbs in proper perspective and avoid being carried away by the editor's own occasional irrelevancies and those championed by the magazine's art director, photo editor or title and blurb writers—especially the art director and photo editor who, presumably because of their artistic nature and certainly because of the nature of their jobs, don't always readily accept the notion that in a magazine the illustrations, photos or otherwise, are to serve, not be served.

The editor then stands her ground, strengthened by the knowledge that the display elements exist to:

1. Draw the reader into the text. That is the elements' major function and their transcending reason for being. It is the major function of *all* the display elements but especially that of the photographs or artwork illustrations and the title and subtitle. The test that the editor must apply to proposed display elements is: "Does this title (or photo or illustration, etc.) make the reader want to read this piece?" If the answer is no, the title (or illustration or blurb, etc.) isn't serving its purpose. If it's not serving its purpose, it needs to be changed or replaced.

2. Illustrate the piece. This function of course applies only to photos, artwork and graphics. They let the reader see what the piece is talking about, which makes the piece more interesting, memorable and effective.

3. Provide visual appeal. The idea is to have the display elements make the layout of a particular piece visually pleasing *and* contribute to the overall visual appeal of the magazine. This function is critically important for most magazines and indeed is of the essence of a magazine.

The Principle of the Unity of Display

To do their job and do it well, the elements of display must work together. Ordinarily when the reader sees the layout of an article's opening page or spread, his eyes land first on either the title or the main illustration (photo or artwork). If it's the title, the reader's eyes then quickly shift to the main illustration. If it's the illustration, the reader's eyes move swiftly to the title. In the moment that the reader takes in those two display elements he should be able to make an instantaneous connection between the two. The connection *must* be obvious—instantly obvious.

The idea of having the major elements of display—the piece's title, subtitle and main illustration—obviously connected and together presenting the reader a single message may be called *the principle of the unity of display.* That principle should be the guiding rule as the editor, usually with the magazine's art director, plans the display of each piece in an issue.

An article in *Reader's Digest* titled "The Secret World of Pandas" opens on a spread, for example, and the illustration is a photo of an adult panda and a cub. The title says "pandas"; the illustration says "pandas"—an instantaneously obvious connection.

In *Sunset* an article titled "Feasts for the eye" opens on a spread and the illustration is a photo of a spectacularly lush vegetable garden. The title says "something lovely to look at" and the illustration says "something lovely to look at." Bingo.

A *Newsweek* article is titled "Queen for 18,250 Days" and opens on a spread. Beside the title are two photos, one of Queen Elizabeth II on the day she was crowned in 1952, and the other of Queen Elizabeth II 50 years later. The title says "a long reign for a queen." The photos show a queen, once young, now grown old and still queen. Title and photos connect.

Now, the necessity for having the title and main illustration support each other by being obviously connected might seem so elementary that it goes without saying. Not so. Editors occasionally forget, ignore or defy the principle. Odd things happen when they do. An article in *New Mexico Magazine* is titled "Mother Julian," and the subtitle reads, "She dished out grub and memories at her boarding house." The article opens on a spread and the illustration is a photo of the article's author, dressed as a cowboy. And so the title says "Mother Julian," but the illustration says "cowboy" or "man." No connection.

A piece from *Reader's Digest* titled "The Doctor Who Conquered a Killer" opens on a single page and the illustration is a photograph of a rural road with farm houses on either side and a horse-drawn carriage coming toward the reader. The title says "doctor" and "conquering a killer." The illustration says—the reader can take his pick: "days of yore"; "rural community"; "Amish farmer"; or whatever else the reader's subjective eye beholds.

An article in *Oklahoma Today* titled "A Tour on the Prairie" opens on a spread and the illustration, extending over three-fourths of the spread, is a photograph of the bend of a river, with trees in the background and a rocky shore in the foreground. The title says "prairie," but the illustration says "river."

The moral of bad examples is: Remember the guiding principle and make the elements connect.

Make It More than Repetition

The goal is not to have the illustration merely repeat the title. Ideally, the illustration should bring something additional to the display, something above and beyond what the title says, something that makes a picture worth a thousand words.

For example, the panda illustration should say more than just "pandas"; it should capture something special about them. The Queen Elizabeth photograph should show not merely her, but should be a shot that shows her in the majestic regalia that makes her look like a queen.

Don't settle for merely an illustration. Look for the illustration that is just right for the display.

Say It Exactly

Another word of caution: Make sure the main illustration says *precisely* what you want it to say. Be certain there's nothing in it that contradicts the title or subtitle or confuses the reader. An article in *Oklahoma Today* titled "The Return of the Wild Horse" is illustrated on the opening spread by a photograph of a running herd of horses. The title is singular; the illustration plural. A title that would fit the photograph better would be "Wild Horses Are Coming Back," or something else that puts "horse" in the plural, since that is what the illustration shows.

Also, although the title says "*wild* horse" (the emphasis is mine), the photograph, as reproduced in the magazine, clearly shows identification numbers on the horses' thighs. So how wild is a horse, the reader has a right to wonder, that has been marked with an ID number? If that's the best shot the editor has to work with, the caption ought to explain the numbers and verify that the horses really are wild and that this isn't a shot of horses that are merely unsaddled.

An article in *The State* magazine is titled "Sentinels of the Sea." The illustration on the opening spread shows a lighthouse against a background of sky and land. There's no sea or water of any kind in the photo. The illustration would support the title much better and would be much more effective if the photo showed the sea, instead of trees, in the background. The photographer should have walked to the other side of the lighthouse and shot toward the water, or the editor should have picked a photo that *was* shot that way, or if the editor was stuck with that one shot, the word "sea" should have come out of the title.

The editor must make the title and illustration agree.

One Is Better than Many

Generally a display works best when it is focused on one message—which is the message of the title and also the main message, or angle, of the piece itself. For example, in the *Reader's Digest* panda piece the title—"The Secret World of Pandas"—and the illustration are obviously linked, and the subtitle—"We may yet save this lovable creature from extinction"—gives the reader an idea of what the piece is going to emphasize about pandas.

In *D* magazine an article titled "Ladies Who Lob" is illustrated with a cartoon that shows a woman with a tennis racket in one hand and a tennis ball in the other, playing tennis. The major display elements, the title and artwork illustration, are quickly connected in the reader's mind, and the subtitle—"For thousands of well-manicured, well-heeled women, Thursdays are tennis league day, and the matches aren't for love"—presents more specifics about the subject of the article.

Both displays, from *Reader's Digest* and *D*, emphasize one idea, which is the main idea of the piece. Both are effective.

In contrast with the one-idea emphasis is a display that ran in *Chesapeake Bay Magazine*. The title of the article is "The Passion of a Lifetime," and the subtitle is "For Hugh Norris, working on the water was more than a family tradition. It was second nature." The opening spread offers three photographs, one showing a boat being launched, one showing a docked boat and one showing a man with a net in his hands sitting on the front porch of a house. The reader isn't given one dominant illustration. His eyes must search the spread for something to focus on and connect with the title—"Passion of a Lifetime." Even after reading the subtitle, which introduces the idea of boats and working on the water, the reader still must sort out the photographs, trying to decide which he should look at first and what do any of them have to do with the title and subtitle. The message is muddled, and the strongest element of display turns out to be the subtitle.

Offering the reader an album of photographs and letting him figure out their relevance is not an effective way to display a piece. The editor should choose a title and subtitle that present a clear message and keep the illustration focused on that same message, letting the title and *the* main illustration support each other, together presenting the piece and its point to the reader.

Subtitles Are Important, Too

Some young editors may take it in their heads that if a piece has the right title on it, there is no need for a subtitle. Not so. In virtually every case, the display needs more come-on than the title provides. Readers are busy and they need reasons to read a piece. Subtitles are supposed to give them reasons.

An opening spread in *New Mexico Magazine* shows a page-and-a-half photograph of a rock formation. Beside the photo is a column of text, the beginning of an article titled "Rock of Ages." There is no subtitle. The piece's title is not the name of the rock formation but is a play on the title and words of an old Protestant hymn. The display cries out for a subtitle that will bring relevance to the reader who has not seen this "rock of ages" and has no idea what or where it is or why he should read about it.

An article in *Reader's Digest* is titled "'Dear IRS'" and the title is printed beneath a cartoon illustration that pictures a woman seated at a desk and pointing toward the outside of the page. No subtitle. What is that piece about? The reader must make herself read the piece to find out.

Going without a subtitle usually happens when title writers get tired or lazy. The editor's job is to tell them—or himself, if he's the culprit—that the display needs more come-on, that the reader needs more reason to read, that subtitles *are* important.

The Cryptic, the Obscure and the Inside-Out

If the reader can't know what the title or the illustration means before reading the piece, something is wrong with the display. Editors who are young or otherwise inexperienced sometimes harbor the mistaken idea that if the title or illustration "teases" the reader—the word is in quotes because those editors merely *think* the reader is teased—the reader will fight to get into the piece and read it so he can decipher the mysterious words or explain the puzzling illustration.

Those editors need to be disabused of that false and harmful premise. Readers want to know what's in the piece—and, more pointedly, what's in it for them—before they decide to spend effort and time reading it. Readers' time is limited; television and newspapers and books and other magazines and other pieces in this issue of this magazine, as well as other demands and distractions, are all competing for the readers' time. The display needs to sell the piece to the reader. Fuzzy or, worse, incomprehensible elements of display run the danger of losing the sale; the reader simply moves on to something more promising.

Fuzzy or incomprehensible display elements fall into three rough categories.

1. The Cryptic. These are display elements with hidden meanings that the reader can never divine merely by looking at them or even studying them. An article in *Modern Maturity* titled "Risky Business" has a subtitle that reads, "All financial planners are not created equal." The artwork illustration shows a disembodied hand holding a pencil that is drawing large stones in a stream, upon which a young couple is standing with arms outstretched to each other. What is that all about? The reader has no way of knowing—or caring.

An article in *Vim & Vigor* magazine is titled "Two Festivals of Light," and the subtitle reads, "Love never dies as long as there is someone who remembers." The stylistic artwork illustration depicts two boys facing each other, their hands clasped and joined, and a dove with a green twig in its bill resting on their hands, all against a background of brightly colored geometric shapes. It's impossible to connect those titles and subtitles with the illustrations beside them.

What do those illustrations mean? Whatever their meanings, they should be instantly apparent to the reader and they are not.

2. The Obscure. These are illustrations that do not illustrate the piece itself; nor do they connect with the other elements of display. Instead, they illustrate some *part* of the piece, often some obscure part—one anecdote buried in the article, perhaps, or one quote or one relatively minor point of the piece. A *Reader's Digest* article titled "Hidden Truths About Hospital Bills" has a subtitle that reads, "Every year patients across the nation are being overcharged for services. You needn't be one of them." The illustration is a drawing of a pair of slip-on slippers made of dollar bills. The illustration does not connect with the title or subtitle. But if you read the text, you'll find meaning for the illustration in the fourth paragraph—and *only* in the fourth paragraph—of a piece that runs four pages in the magazine.

3. The Inside-Out. These are titles especially, but also illustrations and sometimes even subtitles, that do not make sense to the reader until he or she has read the piece. For example, the title on a piece in *Alaska* magazine is "Fannie the Hike." There is no subtitle (although sorely needed), and the opening-page illustration provides no help in understanding the title or the article into which the display is supposed to be inviting readers. The illustration, a still life of objects on a table, is in fact more mysterious than the title. However, if a determined reader will brush past the puzzle of the title and the riddle of the illustration, and force himself upon the text, he will discover that the piece is a profile of a woman known as Fannie the Hike because she walked through the Alaskan wilderness, and each object in the still-life illustration represents some part of her life.

The editor has already read the piece and knows what the words and pictures mean and understands their significance in the story. The display makes sense to the editor because he has read the story. His is the view from the inside.

The reader, on the other hand, is outside looking in. The title, particularly without a subtitle, means nothing to the person who has not already read the piece or does not otherwise know about Fannie the Hike, and the illustration is even more meaningless, if such is possible.

Readers are shopping as they go through the pages of your magazine; they're looking for something that interests them. Editors who want people to read the magazine's content must display the pieces so that readers have a clear idea of what they're going to get when they take time to read them. It's the editor's responsibility to see that readers get that clear idea.

How to Solve the Problems

Each piece scheduled into the magazine must be displayed, and each display is a problem to be solved. Some of the display problems are easy; some are challengingly difficult. On small magazines the editor is usually the chief, perhaps only, solver. On larger magazines the editor often decides on the solutions offered by others. In either case, the editor needs to apply to the solutions his or her own good common sense.

The editor must remember that what is clear to him, or her, is not necessarily clear to the magazine's reader, who has not already read the piece. The editor needs to imagine himself/herself as the reader, to see the content and its display as the reader sees it while browsing through the magazine, hunting something interesting and worthwhile to read. Then the editor needs to give each piece a display that makes it look interesting and worthwhile to the reader.

CHAPTER 9

Planning and Acquiring Photos and Artwork Illustration

O nce a piece has been scheduled into an issue, and sometimes even before, the editor must begin thinking of how it is to be displayed in the magazine. The editor generally has a range of possible ways to illustrate any piece in an issue and once he has settled on an idea for the title—not the exact words necessarily, but the *idea*—he is ready to start the process of determining how the piece should look in the magazine and what is the best possible, or best feasible, way to illustrate it.

Planning Is the Key

There are four steps to achieving good results with illustration: (1) start early; (2) consider alternatives; (3) decide what you want; and (4) insist on what you want. Three of those steps occur during the issue's planning stages, which indicates just how crucial planning is to an effective display of the issue's content and the visual appeal of the magazine.

Planning at the last minute is too often like planning during an emergency—solutions are reached not because they're the best but because they're the best under the circumstances. The editor should give himself plenty of time and thereby avoid emergency conditions. The best time to start planning display in general and illustration in particular is during the planning of the issue itself, or immediately thereafter.

Exploring the Display Alternatives

Should the display be done with photographs or artwork illustration (in graphics-arts parlance, all illustration, including photos, may be referred to as "art"). Or should the display use type only? If the editor's decision is type only—because of the nature of the subject or because photos can't be had and artwork illustration isn't appropriate—the editor can usually leave to the art department the task of selecting a type face and designating the point size, subject to the editor's review. If the decision is other than type only, however, the editor—and perhaps other key staff members—have a number of alternatives to explore.

For example, let's say you, the editor, have scheduled into the magazine a piece that was adapted from a speech by Douglas Wilder, the former Virginia governor who was the only African-American ever elected governor of any state. In this piece Wilder provides some worthwhile, authoritative and highly readable insights into the problems of black families in America. You think it's an important piece and you want to present it appropriately to your magazine's readers.

The question is, as it is for every piece in an issue, how do you display it?

Should you, on the opening page, use a photograph or photographs showing black families or *a* black family? Or should you use a photograph showing the *results* of the problems in black families? Or would it be better to use artwork illustration, perhaps a montage that shows the family *and* the results of the problems? Or maybe a collage that includes both artwork and photos? Ordinarily montages and collages are ineffective because they fail to convey one main message. So if you discard all those possible solutions, what, if anything, is left? Should you think again about handling it with type only?

When you stretch yourself to think beyond the obvious—which is showing in photos or artwork what the piece says in words—you often discover a better way to illustrate and display the piece. With the Wilder piece there is at least one other illustration possibility. Instead of showing what the words of the piece say, the main illustration could show the speaker of the words, the person who has the authority to speak on this subject. In that case, the editor would, in effect, rotate the camera away from the subject and turn it instead on the author, the *source* of the words in the story. *Reader's Digest* effectively solved the problem of illustrating the Wilder piece by using a head shot of Mr. Wilder.

When photography didn't capture—and can't reproduce—the subject or the main event of the piece, artwork illustration can sometimes do what photos can't. Artwork can portray the mood, atmosphere, drama or action that the story describes.

There are other alternatives, too. When there is an action story to be illustrated and you, the editor, decide that a painting or drawing of the action would seem inappropriately melodramatic, even corny, to the reader, you might choose a *suggestion* of the action or scene. A *Reader's Digest* piece titled "Get Back or I Kill Her" has a subtitle that reads, "She figured survival meant doing exactly what her crazed kidnapper commanded, even if it seemed suicidal." The artwork illustration on the opening page is a wide rectangle that shows part of a woman's face, from her eyebrows to the bridge of her nose, capturing an apprehensive look in her eyes.

Or you might choose a photo that shows the main *person* in the story, as in the layout shown in Exhibit 9.1, but make sure that the photo connects with the title and subtitle.

Another possibility might be a photograph that shows the *place* where the story happened or happens. For example, a story on the Nazi Holocaust could be illustrated with a photograph of the Auschwitz concentration camp, or a story on the New York Yankees might be illustrated with a shot of Yankee Stadium.

Another alternative is to build the display around a *symbol* of the article's subject. A *Reader's Digest* piece about why people still immigrate to the United States opens on a single page, and the artwork illustration is a slice of the Statue of Liberty, the symbol of immigration to America.

Photography that says in pictures approximately what the text says in words is often the best and most effective way to illustrate. The layout in Exhibit 9.2, from *Popular Mechanics*, is an example of the effective use of photography on an opening spread. But when such photography isn't possible or affordable or appropriate, the editor can explore alternative illustration by remembering three *S*s and two *P*s: photos or artwork illustrations that show the *S*ource of the piece; or that show a *S*uggestion of the subject; or a *S*ymbol of the subject; or the *P*erson or people included in the subject; or the *P*lace important to the subject.

If all those possibilities fail, there's always type only.

My fingers began
to burn underneath my rings.
Then my feet felt as if they were on fire

13,000 VOLTS!

by Darrell Colter, Gainesville, Georgia

The trip started off as usual. I had loaded my grain-hauling rig with alfalfa meal the day before in Guntersville, Alabama. Then I swung around home in Gainesville, Georgia, and ate supper with Christina, my wife of two years.

After a quick shower, I put on clean jeans, a gray long-sleeved cotton shirt, tan cowboy boots, and my favorite western-style belt with a big silver buckle. I grew up with horses and I've always thought of myself as kind of a ranch hand. That's probably the reason I chose trucking—the next

best thing to riding the open range.

About nine o'clock that January night I kissed Christina good-bye, said a prayer for a safe journey and headed for Whiteville, North Carolina.

Good, clear weather, I thought as I pulled my rig onto the open road. I reached over and cut the radio on to a gospel station. About four years ago, I had started attending church regularly, even driving the van to pick up youngsters for Sunday school. And I was to be ordained a deacon later in the month.

I was excited about the way my life

14 GUIDEPOSTS JULY 1993

Figure 9.1. Reprinted by permission from *Guideposts*.

was going. There was only one thing that troubled me: Christina's brother-in-law, David, a good man I'd grown real close to, still had a broken relationship with the Lord. I guess it was because I'd strayed for a while myself that I wanted so badly for him to find the joy I had—by getting right with God, then leading his family to do the same. I'd tried talking to him, but without success. *If only there were some way I could reach him,* I thought.

I arrived at the packed-dirt parking lot of the Gurganus Milling Company in Whiteville at five in the morning. The company looked to be a family-style operation. A wood-floor porch ran across the front of the main building, providing a ramp for light trucks to load feed, fertilizer, farm equipment and the like. There was no sign of life at that hour, though, so I crawled up onto my bunk in the cab and fell asleep.

It must've been 10:00 A.M. when I heard knocking on the door. The mill's foreman greeted me. "Colter," he said, "there's been a mix-up. The broker should have sent a different

15

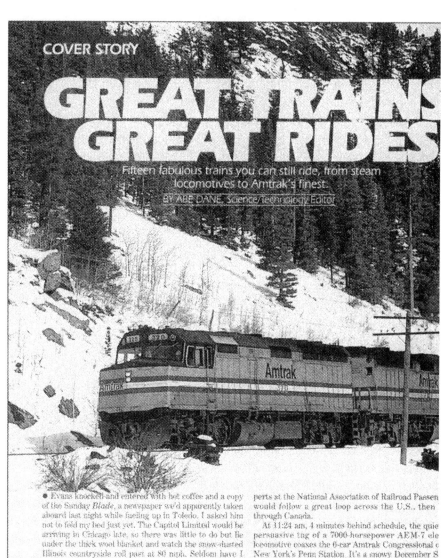

GREAT TRAINS
GREAT RIDES

Fifteen fabulous trains you can still ride, from steam
locomotives to Amtrak's finest.

BY ABE DANE, Science/Technology Editor

● Evans knocked and entered with hot coffee and a copy of the Sunday *Blade*, a newspaper we'd apparently taken aboard last night while fueling up in Toledo. I asked him not to fold my bed just yet. The Capitol Limited would be arriving in Chicago late, so there was little to do but lie under the thick wool blanket and watch the snow-dusted Illinois countryside roll past at 80 mph. Seldom have I found a travel delay less exasperating.

This trip was to be the source of many such revelations. Like most people born since the 1950s, all I knew of long-distance rail travel had come through the wistful recollections of parents and grandparents: heavy silverware and crystal tinkling on crisp dining-car linens, porters shining your shoes while you slept and magnificently powerful machinery hauling it all from city to city.

Hoping to discover what, if anything, remained of those memories, I packed my bags and hit the rails for 11 days last winter. My course, plotted with the help of ex-

perts at the National Association of Railroad Passen would follow a great loop across the U.S., then through Canada.

At 11:24 am, 4 minutes behind schedule, the quie persuasive tug of a 7000-horsepower AEM-7 ele locomotive coaxes the 6-car Amtrak Congressional c New York's Penn Station. It's a snowy December 8 day, and I'm relieved to escape the pre-Christmas fr of Manhattan.

We blaze out from beneath the Hudson River ont fastest, smoothest set of rails in the country. Th where the New York-Washington Metroliners run a mph, racing with the airlines to lure time-consu customers. On weekdays, lawyers and lobbyists fil slender-bodied Amfleet I cars, pounding on their lap Today, we loaf over these silken rails at no more tha mph, but still arrive early in Washington's Union Sta Now beautifully renovated, this soaring beaux-arts

50

Figure 9.2. Reprinted from *Popular Mechanics,* August 1993. Copyright The
Hearst Corporation. All rights reserved.

110

dere is again the country's grandest temple of transation, and a fitting spot from which to launch westd across America.

ix-thousand horsepower from two GM Electromotive 3P4Ls set the Capitol Limited's 14 cars in motion inutes after the appointed time. Along with coaches, gage cars and a diner, the train includes two sleepers my own. Built by Pullman Standard in the 1940s, e are marvels of miniaturization. My roomette, for nple, measures a closet-like 7½ ft. × 3½ ft., yet it ains an upholstered seat wide enough for a sumo stler, a fold-out sink, a toilet, a small closet, a shoe er, an overhead luggage rack and a variety of knobs switches for precise control over climate and lighting. ight, the porter folds down a freshly made-up bed.

ur late arrival in Chicago illustrates a phenomenon too rare on Amtrak. Ironically, this is in part due to railroad's success. Ridership is up, and at the same

time, Amtrak has worked steadily to reduce its dependence on government subsidies by avoiding investment in new equipment. Now, when a breakdown occurs, there isn't much slack in the system to deal with it.

But train travel offers much to distract and soothe all but the most fanatically punctual. My deluxe bedroom aboard one of the Southwest Chief's double-deck Superliner sleepers is one example. Equipped with a bathroom, shower, sink and two bunks, it seemed spacious and comfortable enough to live in indefinitely. The dining car and observation lounge a few steps away allow life to go on pretty much as always, except that you have to reset your watch occasionally to keep up with the time zones.

What is magical is that you are carried effortlessly amid all this luxury through country there's no other way to see without snowshoes. Climbing through the ruggedly beautiful Raton Pass entering New Mexico, I sat down to lunch with a delightful couple, a retired GM executive and

Using Photographs as Artwork

An article on unwed, pregnant college students, who were given pseudonyms in the text, presented an illustration problem for the editor of a campus magazine. Photographs showing the actual students in the story were inappropriate and unavailable. Would the editor have to settle for artwork, a painting or drawing that, by its nature, might diminish the force and authenticity of the article but at least offer some kind of illustration for the opening page? Or was there some other good way to illustrate the piece with photographs?

After exploring the possibilities, the editor decided on photographs that showed a model instead of the students in the story. So long as it is clear to the reader that the model, or other representation of reality, is *not* the real thing, the editor can use photography in the same way he or she would use artwork illustration when photographs of the real thing are inappropriate or unavailable.

Conceptualizing the Opening Display

The editor who wants good results in his magazine's display needs to have in his head—before photo or art assignments are made—a clear picture of what the reader is going to see when her eyes fall on the opening page or spread. Illustration problems should not be left for photographers or illustrators to solve alone, except in an emergency or sheer desperation.

Many magazine editors turn over to the art director the task of conceiving the illustration, an arrangement that lightens the editor's creative load considerably. The wise editor, however, will review the art director's suggested solutions before photo and art assignments are made or illustration is otherwise acquired. The prudent editor will have the art director describe the proposed illustration so that she can see how it connects with the title and subtitle and so she can visualize the effect of the illustration on the opening page or spread. Illustration on the pages following the opening page or spread are important, but illustration on the opening page or spread can be critical.

In other situations, the editor will take a stronger, more direct hand in developing the illustration, particularly on a magazine with a small staff. For the editor who has time to do so and who has a good visual sense, conceiving the illustration, or helping conceive it, can be one of the most enjoyably creative parts of editing a magazine.

How to Find Existing Photographs and Artwork

It's not always necessary to shoot new photographs or commission new artwork illustrations to achieve an effective display. In many cases, existing photos are essential. In other cases, they are good enough. And in nearly all cases they are much easier on the editorial budget than new shots are. The same can be said of artwork illustrations.

Existing photographs come in roughly three categories: (1) news photos, or photos of what once was news, such as, for example, photos of flooded towns along the Missouri River during the Midwest floods of 1993, or shots of the smoking World Trade Center following the terrorist bombing; (2) general illustration, such as photos of the White House, or of a Boeing 747 airliner, or of Babe Ruth; and (3) mood shots, such as photos of the sun setting over the Gulf of Mexico, or of a kitten playing with a rubber mouse, or of a young father pushing his smiling little daughter on a playground swing.

All kinds of such photographs, usually called "stock photographs," are available from photo agencies, from wire service photo files, from newspapers and magazines, from chambers of commerce, airlines, historical associations, public relations departments, museums and libraries, both public and private. For a list of those photo sources, an editor can refer to *Magazine Industry Market Place*, a comprehensive directory of magazine services—editorial and otherwise—available in almost any public library, or *Literary Market Place*, a similar directory serving the book publishing industry, also available in most libraries.

The usual way of finding the photos you want is to telephone or fax the photo agency or other source and tell them what you need. The agency will then ship what it has to you on approval, meaning you pick what you want and immediately return those you don't want. The agency or other source will charge your magazine a fee for a one-time, editorial use of each photo you select for publication.

Not all sources will send you photos on approval. Some will require you or a member of your staff to come in and make your picks at the source's office. If your magazine is located in or near New York City, where most of the photo agencies and other photo sources are, that's not a big problem. If you and your magazine are nowhere near New York, on the other hand, there *is* a problem. It can be solved, however. You can hire, by the hour, a photo researcher who is in New York and who will go to the sources for you. When you need existing photos—or photos you think might exist somewhere—you telephone or fax the photo researcher and tell her what you need, and she'll go to the sources, make selections and send you whatever comes close to what you asked for; you then make your picks and immediately return those you don't want. For a list of such photo researchers, you can again go to *Magazine Industry Market Place* or *Literary Market Place*.

If you see photos you need in your local newspaper or another publication of any sort, don't be shy about asking the publication for permission to use them and for black-and-white prints or color transparencies. Your magazine will be charged a fee, of course, but the fee could be a lot less than what you might have to pay a photographer to shoot an assignment for you. Furthermore, you'll be able to see exactly what you're going to get, instead of hoping for the best from a photographer.

Another source of existing photographs is individuals who have the photos you need in an album or a slide collection at home. If the piece you're trying to illustrate, for example, is a profile, you can ask the profile subject for childhood shots or family shots or shots of the family home or whatever else is appropriate for the piece. Ordinarily people will let you use the photographs they have and ask no more than a careful handling and a prompt return of the pictures.

The imaginative, enterprising editor can save the magazine considerable money, and sometimes acquire photos that otherwise might be out of reach, by using existing shots. Whenever photographs are needed, the thing to do is stop and ask yourself, "Who might already have shots like that?" Then start telephoning.

Existing artwork can also be used, although the opportunities may be far fewer than for photographs. Libraries, museums and archives as well as commercial illustration agencies are all possible sources. To find help, go to *Magazine Industry Market Place* or *Literary Market Place*.

Working with Freelance Photographers and Illustrators

For the editor whose magazine can afford it, the use of freelance photographers and illustrators is the way to go. Their artistry can bring to a magazine's pages powerful, magnetic visual appeal and bring to the reader's eyes and heart great beauty, excitement and drama. They can help tremendously in making the magazine be what a magazine should be.

The really good ones, however, don't work cheap—unless they're still building their portfolios. Good photographers and illustrators, unlike good writers, tend to set their own prices, and for truly first-rate photography an editor or art director could end up paying the photographer more than the magazine paid the writer.

For the editor whose magazine isn't so well-heeled, the trick is to find good *beginning* photographers—and illustrators—just as the budget-minded editor also seeks out freelance writers who do good work but have not been discovered by magazines that can afford to pay top-dollar fees.

Even so, an editor should not be daunted by the fees usually paid to an illustrator or a photographer he would really like to use. There's always a chance that for a certain kind of assignment, or a certain kind of treatment of his work in the magazine, or for a certain kind of magazine, a blue chip illustrator or photographer might work for less. Ask him, or her.

How to Find Good Photographers and Illustrators

The first rule in making assignments to photographers and illustrators is: "Never make an assignment without seeing their work first." So you and/or the magazine's art director or photo editor should keep an eye out for new photographers and illustrators by taking note of credit lines on photos and illustrations published in other magazines. Many illustrators belong to the Society of Illustrators, which is headquartered in New York City and which can tell you how to contact any of their members. Otherwise, phone numbers of illustrators and photographers, or their professional representatives, can ordinarily be obtained from the art director or photo editor of the publication that published their work.

Many freelance photographers and illustrators have professional representatives, or reps, and their reps generally are happy to find new markets for their clients. Reps can show you samples of their clients' work. For a list of artists' and photographers' reps, check *Magazine Industry Market Place.*

There are also photo agencies, such as Magnum and Black Star, that represent photographers and can find one for you in or near almost any location in the world. Those agencies are listed in *Magazine Industry Market Place*.

The Society of Illustrators and the Society of Art Directors each year put on exhibitions displaying their members' work. Those shows, held in New York City, provide a matchless opportunity to see the work of illustrators and collect their names and the names of their agents.

How to Assign Photographs

Before the call goes out to a photographer, a tentative layout should have been made of the article his photographs are to illustrate. The wise editor will leave nothing to chance or purely to the judgment of the photographer, no matter how skilled and experienced. The editor, art director and photo editor, if there is one, should have seen a rough, proposed layout and the editor should have had an opportunity to change the layout if necessary.

After planning the display of the piece, the editor, art director and photo editor will know what the main illustration on the opening page or spread is to show and will know the shape of the photo as it will appear in the issue—a wide horizontal, for example, or a long vertical. The editor, art director and photo editor will also know about how many other shots are to be used in the display and have some idea of what those other shots will show.

Some of the big magazines use story managers, staffers whose job is to shepherd and assist the photographer and make sure he shoots the photos called for in the tentative layout. Small magazines, however, usually depend on the art director or photo editor, or whoever else is going to talk to the photographer and explain the assignment, to know what the photographer is expected to bring back from the shoot. The photographer needs to be told, specifically, what he or she is to shoot; otherwise the display of the piece becomes a function of the photographer instead of the art director.

In cases where one photographer is going to shoot all or most of the pictures for a major article, it is a really good idea to give him a copy of the manuscript, to let him understand what the story is that his photos are going to illustrate.

Photographers, particularly the creative ones, are likely to have ideas of their own about how a story should be shot. A photographer who doesn't have an idea of his own can't be much of a photographer. It is the photographer's pictorial or artistic sense, as well as his craftsmanship with the camera, that your magazine is paying for. So you will expect him to bring creativity to the assignment. But what you must have the photographer understand and must tell him, especially if he hasn't done an assignment for you before, is that he is to shoot it your way first, then shoot it his way if he believes his way is better. Sometimes his way *is* better.

Experienced magazine photographers generally don't need to be told that you want to see *a lot* of shots. If the assignment is to shoot the mayor on the roof of city hall, overlooking the city, you and the art director and photo editor will want not one or two such shots, but a dozen or more. You want to be able to *select*, not settle. You want to be able to pick a really good shot; you don't want to have to use whatever's there. So if the photographer has never done an assignment for your magazine, make sure he is told to shoot his brains out—and give you *rolls* of film, not just a few frames.

Because the layout has already been planned, you and the art director and the photo editor will know which shots are to be in color and which in black-and-white. Make sure the photographer gets that information. Tell him that when in doubt, shoot color. Color can always be converted to black-and-white, but going the other way is a bit difficult.

It's a good idea to let the photographer know that what you are expecting from him are contact sheets in the case of black-and-white and transparencies in the case of color. You want to see *the entire take—* not just the shots that the photographer likes. After you and the art director and photo editor have made your black-and-white selections, the photographer can then make the appropriate prints.

When releases are necessary to avoid the possibility of an invasion of privacy lawsuit from someone who is unavoidably included in a photograph, the photographer should get a release from that person. A photographer without substantial magazine experience may need to be reminded to get releases.

And of course the photographer needs to be given a deadline, the shorter the better.

Freelance photographers often require a day rate, which they or their agency sets, plus expenses. Photographers without an agency or an agent are more likely to be flexible about their rates or expected fees. When money's no object, of course, your magazine pays what it takes to get the person—and, you trust, the quality—that you want for your magazine. When money is, or might be, a problem, you must have the magazine's art director or photo editor tell the photographer what the magazine can afford to pay, then let the photographer decide whether he wants to do a particular assignment for that particular price.

One other thing: Good, dependable, agreeable photographers are invaluable to a magazine and pure joy to an editor, art director and photo editor. Those photographers who show themselves to be so ought to be told every once in awhile that you, the editor, love their work.

How to Assign Artwork Illustrations

It is vital that the illustrator see in his mind the illustration as the editor and/or the art director have planned it, since the illustrator, unlike the photographer, will deliver *one* picture, not many from which the editor may choose the exactly right one. So the editor or art director—whoever talks to the illustrator to make the assignment—*must* know what the illustration is to show and must describe it to the illustrator.

Like the photographer, naturally, the illustrator is expected to bring his own artistry to the assignment. He is expected not to merely render the illustration as described, but to add something to the essentials of the illustration. So the illustrator needs to know what the illustration is to show, but he or she needs freedom to make it a piece of art, not a diagram.

The illustrator also needs to be told the shape the illustration should be and, if type is to be superimposed, where the uniformly light or dark area should be.

Some illustrators, after having the assignment explained, will submit several pencil sketches showing alternative ways to compose the elements of the illustration. The editor and the art director can then pick the one they like best, and that's the way the finished illustration will look.

Give the illustrator a reasonable amount of time to complete the illustration. Ordinarily you can tell him when you need it and the illustrator will tell you if he or she can do it by then. Good illustrators often have a backlog of assignments, and it may take them a while to do yours.

You can expect an experienced illustrator to have a more or less standard fee, but if it's a little rich for your magazine's budget, for the right client or right assignment, he might work within your magazine's limitations. An illustrator without a lot of experience will be looking for additions to his portfolio as well as some money and he might leap at an opportunity to do a big, gutsy, color illustration for a price your magazine can afford.

CHAPTER 10

Titles and Subtitles

Titles come in as many varieties as the pieces they introduce. Some make shocking statements, some deliver warnings, some pose questions. Some are short, some long, some very long. Some are poetic or romantic or dramatic or starkly straightforward. Some are built on a pun, an allusion or alliteration. There are all kinds.

It's not their *kind*, however, that makes them good or bad, effective or not effective. It's what they say to the reader. Titles are good when they are readable in their own right, and effective when they draw the reader into the text, which is their major reason for being.

To be good and effective, a title should be:

1. Eloquent. What it says should be said well. Its words should be precise, its language appropriate, its message clear, its construction flawless.

2. Provocative. It should provoke interest and compel the reader to read the text.

3. Consistent with the tone of the story. If the story is serious, the title should be serious. If the story is lighthearted, the title should be lighthearted. If the story is absurd, the title should be absurd.

4. A concise description of the story. A title should not be about *something* in the piece. It should be about the message of the entire piece. It should go to the heart of the story.

5. Connected to the subtitle and the illustration. It should be *obviously* connected. The title, subtitle and main illustration should support one another, together make one statement and together impel the reader into the story.

The Good, the Bad and the Ugly

Here are some good and, in one editor's judgment, effective titles.

A profile of a worker at a university's sewage treatment plant describes in vivid and pungent detail the place, the process and the man's job. The title:

THE GUY WITH THE CRAPPIEST JOB ON THE CAMPUS

An article about the Adirondack Museum and its collection of antique boats, housed in an old boathouse, is titled:

THE BEST LITTLE OARHOUSE

An article about losing unsightly and unhealthy fat is titled:

HOW TO GET RID OF YOUR POTBELLY

An article about black cats and a family that prefers them is titled:

BLACK CATS, BAD LUCK. NOT!

An article about an unmarried high school student's struggle to decide whether she should keep her baby or give it up for adoption is titled:

THE FOREVER DECISION

An article that details what happens when a driver is stopped for driving while intoxicated is titled:

WHAT YOU CAN EXPECT IF YOU'RE STOPPED
FOR DRUNK DRIVING

An article about a young teacher's eye-opening discovery of how little college students know is titled:

ISN'T J. EDGAR HOOVER THE GUY WHO INVENTED
THE VACUUM CLEANER?

An article that shows what it's like to be confined to a wheelchair is titled:

A DAY OF LIFE IN A WHEELCHAIR

One of the biggest mistakes that title writers make is saying too little in the title. Brevity may be the soul of wit—and sometimes eloquence—but usually it is merely vague. Here are some bad examples.
An article about bird-watching had this title:

EXTRAORDINARY!

An article about the javelina, a wild hog that inhabits the Southwest, is titled:

SOUTHERN ROUGHNECK

An article about ice storms and their effects on nature is titled:

SILVER STORM

An article about the developing medical specialty that treats sports injuries and ailments has this title:

SPORTS MEDICINE

Worse than those say-nothing titles, which serve as mere labels instead of provocative titles, are titles that are not only vague but mysterious as well. Here are some ugly examples.
For an article about flamingoes, the title was:

DE FILLYMINGO MON!

For an article about a plant called devil's club, the title was:

A HORRID WEAPON THAT CURES ALL?

An article about rubber-rafting on the Alsek River in Alaska was titled:

THE RIVER'S EDGE

Making matters worse—for the effectiveness of the titles and for the readers—none of those ugly titles were accompanied by a major illustration that made their meaning clear to readers.

How to Write Good, Effective Titles

The best starting place for writing good, effective titles is a thorough understanding of what a title is meant to do. A title is supposed to be much more than a label for the story. Its purpose is very similar to that of a headline on an advertisement: It's supposed to arrest the reader's attention, arouse his interest, make him want to read more and move him into the text, where the information is.

From that starting place a title-writing editor takes several steps to arrive at a good, effective title. Here are the steps:

1. Decide that writing titles is not a chore but a challenge. Many editors even think it's fun. They have learned to relish the work in the same way that a crossword puzzle devotee delights in solving a crossword puzzle, especially a tough one. If attitude isn't everything, it's certainly one of the things necessary to succeed at writing titles. Make sure you've got a good one.

2. Allow plenty of time. Writing titles and subtitles can eat up hours, and when you know that a deadline is close or there are other pressing matters to attend to, there might be a tendency for an editor to bang out something that will pass as a title and then look at it and say, "Good enough." What you want for your magazine and its readers are titles that are good, not good enough. Relax and settle in for a long, enjoyable session. The titles will be the better for it.

3. Know the story. If you haven't read the whole story, read it. If you read it a few days ago, read it again. Make sure you have the main message—the angle—clear in your head. You can't write a decent title and subtitle without knowing what the story is, what it is saying to the reader.

4. Capture the message. Get it down in words on your computer screen or on paper. Make a statement or ask a question, but project the main idea to the reader in a few words.

Sometimes a question works better than a statement. It can be more provocative than a statement, forcing the reader to read the text to find the answer. It can also avoid making an editorial statement. (Editorial statements are appropriate for an editorial, but usually not otherwise.) Examples:

WHAT'S GOING TO HAPPEN TO OUR
    PAROCHIAL SCHOOLS?
IS THE SEX REVOLUTION OVER?

The titles raise the questions, but do not make the statements. Readers have to read the stories to find the answers.

5. Capture the tone. Make the title match the piece. A big, heavy piece needs a big, heavy title. A fun piece needs a fun title. A how-to piece needs a how-to title. Et cetera.

6. Create a selection. Don't stop at one title. Write a batch of them. Keep them all on your screen or copy paper. Write down everything that comes to your mind, as fast as it comes. Get a lot of title possibilities out in front of you.

7. When stumped, try a whole new approach. Go back to the manuscript and look for a key sentence or phrase or quote that will sum up the main message of the piece, then try making a title of it, such as:

IF YOU WANT A FRIEND IN WASHINGTON,
GET YOURSELF A DOG

Or:

"GET BACK OR I KILL HER"

Or try making the title ask a question:

IS THIS THE MAN WILL ROGERS NEVER MET?

Try joining two key ideas with a colon or dash, such as:

THE NIGHTMARE OF AIDS: TWO VICTIMS TELL THEIR
STORIES.

Other ways to get past the stump: Take a break; go to lunch; go to the
restroom; skip the problem title for now and go to the next one, then
return to the tough one after you've written an easier one.

8. Don't worry about length or space. Unless your magazine's pages
are divided into rigid, newspaper-style columns, don't think of writing
titles to fit a space. Think instead of writing the best possible title, using
as few or as many words as it takes. Let the art director worry about fitting it into the layout.

9. Edit and refine. Once you've got the key words down on your
screen or copy paper, work them around, add to them or subtract from
them, make substitutions, say it smoothly and clearly, say it to get the
proper effect, keep working till the title is just right.

10. Start thinking about the subtitle.

Some Words About Subtitles

The subtitle's job is to elaborate on the title and to provide come-on
for the reader by giving him more information about what's in the text
and hinting at what he will discover if he reads the piece.

Practically all titles need subtitles, either to expand on the idea in the
title or to make the title make sense to the reader. For example, here is a
title that ran above a piece in a national magazine:

THE BIG RED HEN AND THE DEVIL'S HOOFPRINTS

What does that title mean? What is the story about? What promise or
come-on does it hold for the reader? The piece presented no subtitle to
help the reader understand or give him a reason to spend time reading
the piece. Furthermore, the cartoon illustration showed only a woman
and a girl driving in a car, which contained no clue to the title's meaning
or the piece's subject.

Such throwaway titles, which are intended to arrest the reader's attention and arouse his interest through curiosity, *especially* need a subtitle.
The editor cannot count on the reader being so curious about the title's
unknown meaning that he or she will dive into the text to discover it.
Throwaway titles are fun and are singularly appropriate on a light piece,

but they require subtitles that give the reader more information about the piece and more reason to read it. Here's an example.

The throwaway title:

POP TARTS, SOAP OPERAS AND THE STAR-SPANGLED BANNER

The elaborating subtitle:

In the eyes of foreigners, we Americans have some strange tastes and some weird and wacky ways of living.

The subtitle doesn't deaden the title; it maintains its tone and elaborates on the title, so the reader has some idea of what the piece is about and what he will get out of the piece if he reads it.

Straightforward pieces with tricky titles require subtitles that are much more explicit than their titles. For example:

The title:

UNPEACEABLE KINGDOM

The subtitle:

The battle over animal rights pits pet lovers against scientists, emotion versus reason. The animal advocates say they want to save helpless dogs and cats. The scientists say they want to save humanity.

A straightforward piece with a straightforward title also needs an elaborating subtitle that provides explicitness and promise to the reader. For example:

The title:

BIG RED: RUDDY RIVER OF THE NORTH

The subtitle:

The historic stream sculpts some of Texas's most rugged landscapes before forming the sinuous border with Oklahoma.

Ordinarily, subtitles are written as complete sentences, with normal capitalization and lower-casing of letters and normal punctuation, including periods. Titles, on the other hand, if not all caps, usually (but not necessarily) capitalize the initial letters of all major words and are not necessarily complete sentences and do not use periods.

What to Avoid When Writing Titles

Editors should be aware of the most common ills and temptations of title writing and strive to avoid them. Title writers should avoid:

■ *Gerund titles.* For example, avoid writing titles like these:

WRITING GOOD, EFFECTIVE TITLES
FISHING THE CALOOSAHATCHEE
BRINGING BABY HOME
THE WINNING OF THE WEST

Such titles serve mostly as identifying labels for the pieces they introduce and do not say anything specific to the reader. They would be better and more effective if they read like this instead:

HOW TO WRITE GOOD, EFFECTIVE TITLES
THE ADVENTURE OF FISHING THE CALOOSAHATCHEE
BRINGING BABY HOME: WHAT EVERY NEW MOTHER
    NEEDS TO KNOW
HOW THE WEST WAS WON

Make titles say something to the reader.

■ *Inside-out titles.* Avoid titles that aren't clear or don't make sense to the reader until he or she has read the story. The editor must remember that, unlike the title writer, the reader sees the title first, then the piece, whereas the title writer sees the piece first, then the title. Magazines are to be edited for their readers, not their editors.
■ *Cuteness.* What may seem cute to the title writer could easily seem silly, corny or repellingly amateurish to the reader. The safest way to avoid offending is to steadfastly resist the temptation to be cute—a temptation that comes to all title writers from time to time.

■ *Giving everything away.* The idea of the title and subtitle is to make the reader want to read the text. It is *not* to summarize the piece and let the reader feel he has read the piece by reading the title and subtitle. So don't give the story away. Don't tell the reader everything. Tell enough to make him want to read more. Let him see what he's going to get from the piece. But be careful not to give him a reason for *not* reading the text.

CHAPTER 11

Blurbs and Captions

While titles and subtitles, along with illustration, are the major elements of display on an article's opening page or spread, blurbs and captions, along with illustration, are the major elements of display on the pages following the opener or on the jump pages.

The Purposes of Blurbs and How to Write Them

Blurbs have three purposes and are used by the editor or art director for one or more of them. They are used to: (1) stop the reader who is skimming through the magazine and draw him or her into the text; (2) break up the grayness of the text type or otherwise add to the visual appeal of a page or spread; and (3) act as filler material, so that the piece fills the space allotted for it.

The best blurbs are those that provoke interest in the text and provide visual appeal as well. They ordinarily are a phrase or sentence (sometimes called "quote-outs"), possibly two, pulled from the text and blown up. They are usually either the words of the piece's author or a quote from one of the piece's sources.

To write them, the blurb writer should search the text for *provocative* quotes or statements. Ordinarily they need to be concise and so may have to be edited. If the blurb is a quote from one of the piece's sources, the blurb writer must be careful to avoid disturbing the source's meaning. If in the blurb words must be deleted from the quote for the sake of conciseness or clarity or to avoid repetition, the blurb writer should indicate the dropped words with an ellipsis (...) so the quote in the blurb will match the quote in the text, except for the omitted words shown by the ellipsis. For example, here's the way the text read:

> "Abstinence is great," she said. "It's cheap, it's free, it works, it keeps you from getting any sexually transmitted diseases, and in a lot of ways it keeps a lot of individuals from getting so involved in relationships that a breakup is horribly traumatic. No one says it's easy, especially at the age most college students are. But there are ways to be intimate with people without having sex with them."

Here's the way the blurb read:

> 'Abstinence is great. It's free, it works. ... There are ways to be intimate with people without having sex.'

If the blurb is not a quote, but is instead the words of the author of the piece, the blurb writer is free to condense or otherwise edit the statement to achieve conciseness or clarity in the blurb. For example, the text of a profile of botanist David Hall read as follows:

> In court the defense attorney asked Hall if it was true that the plants on the blanket could grow in the areas where the defendant claimed he had picnicked. Hall said they could, but they would have to be between three and ten feet tall to bloom and produce the seeds found on the blanket.
>
> That was the key: The plants at the alleged picnic sites had not grown to that size, whereas the ones at the alleged rape site had.
>
> On that evidence, Hall said, the man was convicted and sentenced to 44 years for sexual assault and 44 years for kidnapping.

The blurb taken from that section of the text read:

Because of Hall's testimony, the man was convicted and sentenced to 44 years for sexual assault and 44 years for kidnapping.

The editor should strive to have blurbs that appear on a certain page or spread come from sections of text that also appear on that page or spread. The blurb and the text from which it comes, in other words, should be on the same page, or spread.

Kinds of Captions and What to Say in Them

Captions come in a variety of kinds. Here are some of the most popular.

Label

This is the bare-bones kind of caption. It says no more than it has to. If the photo is of Mickey Mantle, the caption reads: Mickey Mantle.

Description

This kind of caption describes what the picture shows. When a photo's contents need identification or explanation, so the reader knows what he is looking at, the description kind of caption is a good one to use. Example: The photo shows racehorses running on a racetrack. The caption reads, "Thoroughbreds make a final dash to the finish line at The Downs at Santa Fe."

Picture Plus

This kind of caption not only tells the reader what's in the picture, it gives him some other information as well. Example: The photo shows a young man on a lakeshore, bending over and reaching for something at the water's edge. The caption reads, "Graduate student Grant Hokit grabs Cascades frog in Oregon's Scott Lake, where they can still be found. No one knows why they are gone from some lakes, not others. Mountains in back are the Three Sisters."

Storyteller

In this kind of caption the reader is told something about the scene depicted, about how the subject of the picture fits into the story that is told in the text. Example: The artwork illustration shows several men in conquistador uniforms about to confront a large group of Indians wearing headdresses. The caption reads, "An unprovoked massacre occurred during Cortes' absence, when a Spanish garrison fell upon Aztecs celebrating a religious festival, cutting them to pieces. The attack ignited war that led to the empire's ruin."

ID

This is a straightforward, no-frills, no-fooling-around, only-what-you-need-to-know identification, left to right or clockwise, of the subjects of the photograph. Example: The photo shows two women and three men standing side by side outside the White House. The caption reads, "House sitters: Ruth Marcus (*The Washington Post*), Matthew Cooper (*U.S. News & World Report*), Gwen Ifill (*The New York Times*), Mark Halperin (ABC), and Jeffrey Birnbaum (*The Wall Street Journal*) at the West Wing entrance."

Oblique

This kind of caption doesn't really identify the subject of the picture. Instead, it tells the reader something about the subject, and the reader is led to conclude that the person or object in the photo is the one mentioned in the caption. Example: The photo is a head-and-shoulders of a portrait of an aristocratic-looking man in 18th century clothes. The caption reads, "King George III helped make Wedgwood famous."

Let's Pretend

Every editor is allowed to have favorites, and this kind is this author's *least* favorite. The caption pretends that the photo is something other than a posed shot or a shot otherwise set up by the photographer. It pretends purpose or activity on the part of the subject when in fact the subject was merely posing. It also pretends that the reader doesn't have enough sense to know it's a posed shot. Example: The photo shows a woman in a hospital bed, holding an infant and smiling into the camera, and close beside her, halfway in the bed, is a young boy, also smiling into the camera. The caption reads, "Welcome to the world: Mom Pam Eward of Hamilton, Ill., and son Jarrod, 2, greet newborn baby Grant."

Combo

This is an all-in-one kind of caption that talks about not just one picture but several on the same page or spread—sometimes even on the preceding or following page.

Which kind is best? Probably the kind that works best in a particular layout. However, bearing in mind that captions are elements of display and not merely picture identifiers, the editor is likely to conclude that the most effective captions are probably those that identify the subject of the picture *and* give the reader some additional come-on, to entice him or her into the text. To do a really good job with such captions, it sometimes is necessary for the caption writer to gather additional information about the subject in the photograph, information above and beyond that provided by the author in the article.

One of the best rules about caption writing is, allow enough time to write good ones. Carefully constructed captions can contribute to the reading enjoyment that readers get from the magazine. Captions written as a mere afterthought are not likely to provide such enjoyment.

When Captions Aren't Necessary

There are occasions when captions not only aren't needed but may look a little silly if you put them in. When the subject of the photo or artwork is either well known to the reader or is obviously the person or object that appears in the title, there often is no need to use a caption.

CHAPTER 12

The Table of Contents

Among editors, thoughts about the table of contents are apt to range from a necessary evil to a waste of space. There are good reasons for having one, however, no matter how the editor may view its purpose in the magazine.

What's It For Anyway?

One way for the editor to view the table of contents is to see it as a *promotion* of the articles in an issue. With that promotion purpose in mind, an editor will take an entire page or more to call the reader's attention to each article in the issue, repeating the title and subtitle from the display of the piece or writing a new, more provocative version of them, and running a photograph or other illustration from the piece, along with the author's byline, the photographer's credit and, of course, the number of the page on which the piece begins.

Other promotion-minded editors will list each article and emphasize one or two of them.

Many editors, on the other hand, see the table of contents as a *directory*, giving little or no thought to promoting the content other than to list the titles of the articles. The directory approach usually means listing not only the issue's articles but other content as well.

The most popular approach to the table of contents, however, judging by the number and kinds of magazines that use it, is a combination of directory and promotion. Some, as *Reader's Digest* once did, use their cover as their table of contents, making it more a directory than a promotion. Others, such as *Money* magazine, which may give an entire spread to it and lavishly illustrate it, make it more promotion than directory. Most, however, like *Boca Raton* magazine, seem to blend directory and promotion in equal parts (see Figure 12.1).

Still, there is no escaping the feeling of some editors that giving as much as an entire page to the table of contents is a waste of precious editorial space. Editors who think that way manage to place something besides the table of contents on the contents page. *Ireland of the Welcomes*, the magazine of the Irish Tourist Board, for example, tastefully squeezes onto the contents page the magazine's logo and issue date, a message from the chairman of the Irish Tourist Board, a photograph of the chairman, a list of the Irish Tourist Board's offices around the world, a list of photo and illustration credits, other acknowledgements, a squib about the cover, a reproduction of the issue's cover *and*, by the way, the table of contents.

Audubon magazine doesn't use so many elements on the contents page but provides more promotion of the issue's articles while at the same time forcing the table of contents to share the page with the masthead, the publisher's statement and a cover squib (Figure 12.2).

One of the most grudging concessions of editorial space to the table of contents can be found in *AutoWeek*, which gives less than a third of its contents page to a list of the issue's contents and uses most of the rest of the page for editorial material, including illustration (Figure 12.3).

The Rationale for Running a Table of Contents

When the editor uses cover lines to promote certain pieces in an issue, he or she assumes that the reader will read them and be drawn to one or more of those articles in the magazine. If, for example, a set of cover lines says "New Ways to Stop Smoking," and a reader wants to find that article in the issue, she ordinarily has only two ways of finding it. She either flips through the magazine, searching for the display, or

Figure 12.1.   Reprinted by permission from *Boca Raton* magazine.

she turns to the table of contents and looks for the appropriate title and page number.

In that case, the magazine performs a service to its readers by providing a table of contents that quickly locates the desired article. That service, which makes it easier for the reader to enjoy the magazine, is a good reason for publishing a table of contents as a directory. Also, when

Figure 12.2.   Reprinted by permission from *Audubon.*

a reader has to lay the issue aside before she finishes reading a particular article, whether it is promoted on the cover or not, the table of contents helps her find the piece again when she has time to return to it. In a magazine the size of, say, *Good Housekeeping*, which could run more than 180 pages in an issue, help in finding a particular piece is usually a

Figure 12.3.   Reprinted by permission from *AutoWeek*.

necessity. The table of contents also helps the reader who has read a particular article and wants to refer to it or reread it later.

A second rationale for a table of contents, applicable to its use as promotion, concerns the reader who by habit turns to the contents page to see what's interesting in an issue, instead of flipping pages and browsing through the whole magazine. The table of contents in that case becomes like a second cover, advertising *all* the pieces in an issue—and at the same time letting the reader know where the pieces are in the issue.

Making a Choice

If the editor has a choice, he will pick the style of table of contents best suited to his taste and beliefs about the readers' needs and reading habits. If the editor does not get to choose, he goes along with the magazine's traditional way of doing it—which, oddly enough, the readers may actually like.

Despite all the variables and allowances for the philosophy and taste of the editor, there is one absolute concerning the table of contents. This absolute must be applied to every issue of every magazine. It's simply this: Always make sure that the page numbers in the table of contents coincide with the page numbers of the pieces themselves. Except for that one rule, the editor usually has a lot of leeway to shape the table of contents to his or her own preferences.

CHAPTER 13

Letters to the Editor and Standing Features

The wise editor will strive to build reader loyalty to the magazine, which in the case of consumer magazines usually means substantial renewal rates and in all cases means that readers read and enjoy the magazine—which is the editor's highest goal and the object of all his labors.

Two devices that the editor can use to help create and develop reader loyalty are (1) letters to the editor, which readership surveys consistently show to be one of the most popular parts of any publication, and (2) standing features, which help create an identity for the magazine and rapport with the readers.

The Voice of the Readers

Newspapers and magazines alike generally believe it's important to give readers an opportunity to have their say, to talk back to writers and editors or make comments of any kind. For many magazines the publication of letters to the editor has proved an excellent way to provide that opportunity. In the letters columns, readers get a chance to disagree with published material, including letters from other readers, or present their own knowledge of a subject, or speak their mind about anything relevant to the magazine or its content. Letters to the editor allow a dialogue between the magazine and its readers, and being able to hear what other readers are saying is what makes letters to the editor so appealing to the readership in general. The columns of letters become a public forum, the livelier the better, open to all readers.

Here are some guidelines the editor may follow in creating or developing a letters-to-the-editor column.

Encourage Readers to Write   It's a good idea to run a box or other kind of notice in each issue, inviting readers to write and telling them how to submit letters and where to send them. Tell them whatever you want them to know about the magazine's policy concerning letters to the editor—maximum length, typewritten, double-spaced, signed by the sender and so forth. A good place for the notice is at the end of the letters column. If e-mail letters are accepted, give the magazine's e-mail address.

Require Reader's Full Name, Address and Phone Number on Letter   You will want the letter's authenticity to be verifiable. Even though in special circumstances the letter writer's identity may be withheld when the letter is published, you will want his or her name and other identifying and verifying information about the letter writer.

Check the Letter's Authenticity when Appropriate   Checking is appropriate when you have any doubts or suspicions about the letter or its writer. Telephone the purported author and verify that he or she did indeed write the letter. Don't publish it if doubts remain.

Edit the Letters when Necessary   All letters should be subject to light editing, especially editing that reduces length or eliminates repetition or deletes potentially libelous statements, objectionable language or unintelligible remarks. It's a good idea to mention in the published notice that invites readers to write that letters are subject to editing.

Balance the Letters   Don't shy away from letters critical of the magazine or its content. Critical letters are often more readable than letters of approbation. When choosing which letters to publish, always remember that the letters column is supposed to be *readable*. Letters written in reaction to something the magazine published may be divided between approving and denunciatory. Juxtapose letters containing opposing reactions so readers can see and enjoy the differences of opinion, identifying with one or the other.

Publish an Editor's Reply when Appropriate   Those appropriate times occur when:

■ *Acknowledging a correction of fact.* When a reader or an authority of some sort writes to correct an error published by the magazine, the editor may want to acknowledge a correction that sets the record straight.

■ *Acknowledging a different point of view.* A reader who was involved in an event or situation described in a story may be able to shed new light on the event or situation, presenting facts known only to that reader and not available to the author of the story.

■ *Contesting reader disagreements.* Letter-writing readers who challenge facts as published in the magazine aren't always right, of course. When the magazine did have the facts straight, the objecting reader needs to be told so. The same goes for letters that otherwise protest something in the magazine; if the editor stands by what the magazine or its authors have done or said, let the readers know it.

Depending on the letter writer's criticism and the tone of his letter, the editor's reply may be either tactful or tart. The readers of some magazines, such as *Car & Driver*, seem actually to prefer tart, sock-it-to-'em replies from the editor when the letter writer has it coming.

■ *Providing additional information.* Letter writers who want to know more about something relatively minor mentioned in a story deserve a reply that, if possible, gives them the additional information they seek. The editor should provide it in a reply, allowing other readers, who may have wondered but did not write a letter, to see it, too.

Publish the Letters in the Same Place Every Issue   The front of the magazine is the traditional location for letters to the editor, but wherever the editor chooses to place them, the reader should be able to turn to that spot each issue and find the letters, which often are the first thing a regular reader reads in an issue. Therefore, finding them in an issue should be made as easy for the reader as is possible.

Building a Family of Features

Standing features should be like old friends to the magazine's regular readers—familiar, dependable, enjoyable. They should be such that readers look forward to being reunited with them each month, or as often as the magazine is published. They should be among the constants of the magazine, helping anchor each issue to the expectations of the regular reader.

Many standing features are something other than text pieces; they are lists or tabular material or puzzles or photographs or graphics or something else nontextual. However, many more *are* text pieces—essays, advice columns, travelogues, how-to pieces, nostalgia pieces, letters from the editor or from the publisher, etc. Whatever the standing features are, to find an enduring spot in the reader's heart, they should:

1. Be Readable. To be readable, standing features should bear the marks of any good piece of writing: They should present characters, at least one (which may be the feature's author), with whom readers can readily identify; they should contain anecdotes (at least one), descriptive detail and lively quotes—all the elements of good writing. The editor must be careful that a standing feature does not become merely an ego service for its author; it should always be, first of all, a treat for the reader.

2. Have a Message. They should say something to the reader. Ideally, they should speak to the reader's heart as well as his or her head; they should let the reader *feel* as well as know. In every case, they should make a point and give the reader something to go away with.

3. Reflect the Readership as Well as the Magazine. Standing features need to be something that readers easily identify with and at the same time they need to be something that conveys the concept of the magazine to the readers. It doesn't matter whether the publication is a consumer, trade or public-relations magazine, the idea and purpose of standing features remain the same. The ideal feature binds the readers together and engenders good feelings toward the magazine.

CHAPTER 14

The Cover— A Magazine's Most Important Page

For the reader, the cover is where the magazine starts, the page that the reader, whether subscriber or newsstand buyer, sees first, and one form of logic would have placed this chapter first in this book.

For the editor and the rest of the magazine's staff, however, the cover develops while the issue is still in its formative stages and sometimes is not finally decided until the issue is nearly complete. So following the sequence in which the issue is ordinarily put together, and with most of the editorial elements of the magazine having been handled in earlier chapters, we are now ready to move to the magazine's *piece de resistance* page—the cover.

The editor of an existing, successful magazine will inherit the general design and look of the cover from his or her predecessor. On the other hand, the editor of a start-up magazine or a magazine that needs drastic change will want to call in the magazine's art director and/or an outside designer to come up with a logo and prototypical cover design that will best suit the magazine, its audience, the editor and the art director. The cover is not an area to be treated offhandedly or parsimoniously. It presents the magazine's image and makes a statement about the magazine, in the same way one's clothes and appearance say something about the person.

Functions of the Cover

Besides its use as a protective covering for the pages of the magazine, the cover has two integrally related functions: (1) sell the magazine and (2) do so by selling the issue's content.

In the case of single-copy sales, the cover is intended actually to sell the magazine, to attract the browsing potential reader and cause him or her to lift the magazine from the sales rack, examine it, buy it and read it. In the case of subscribers to the magazine, the cover is intended, in effect, to sell the issue. Most magazine subscribers subscribe to more than one magazine, and those magazines compete for the subscriber's attention in much the same way that magazines compete on the racks of a supermarket or drugstore. The magazine that does not call its subscriber's attention to itself and that consequently goes unread is likely to have its subscriber ask herself at renewal time, "Do I really need this magazine?" and get a "no" answer in reply. Each issue should in effect resell the magazine to the subscriber, reinforcing her original decision to subscribe and maintaining a prominent place in the subscriber's reading time. Then when the renewal notice arrives, the subscriber will realize how important the magazine is to her and be more likely to renew her subscription.

So it doesn't matter whether the reader is a subscriber or a newsstand buyer, for in either case the cover has the same two functions, one naturally following the other—sell the content, sell the magazine.

With so important a role to perform, it is no exaggeration to call the cover the most important page in the magazine. And it is no misallocation of time, effort or money for the editor to treat the cover as the magazine's most important page.

Picking a Cover Story

A cover will generally promote more than one of the issue's pieces of content, but most magazines prefer to pick one of the dozen or more pieces in an issue and make it the focus of the cover.

Another way of focusing the cover on one piece in the issue is to make one piece the *only* piece that is advertised on the cover, as in Figure 14.1.

Sometimes the editor will avoid focusing on one piece and instead make two or more pieces share prominence on the cover. In my view, *one* main cover piece is preferable, since treating two or more pieces

Figure 14.1.   Reprinted from *Orange & Blue Magazine.*

equally dilutes the message and effectiveness of each. In picking one cover piece, the question inevitably is, *Which one?* Another question, just as important, is, *On what basis should the choice be made?*

The answer to the question "Which one?" of course comes from the editor, perhaps together with key members of the magazine's staff, who chooses from the content available for a particular issue. A general answer, however, applies to the question of a basis for deciding on a cover story. Generally, five considerations govern the selection of a cover story:

1. Strength. The cover story ought to be a well written piece that reflects thorough reporting and contains solid documentation, ample details, illustrative examples and smooth, clear prose. It ought to be well and logically organized, with an effective lead, a clear justifier, a make-sense sequence of presentation of the material and an appropriate conclusion. It should be, ideally, the *strongest* piece in the issue.

2. Importance. The story's subject should have significance, for the public at large or at least for the magazine's readers. What the piece says should *matter* to the magazine's audience.

3. Length. If the piece is important, it should have length as well as strength. It should *look* like a major piece—or it will be diminished by comparison with longer, more substantial-looking pieces in the same issue.

4. Promotability. It's possible for a subject to be important without being especially promotable. Registering to vote, for example, is important, but not very promotable. It's not the sort of subject that readers will want to pay money to read about. Ideally, the cover story should be about a subject that the reader will be eager to read about, that a newsstand browser will be willing to pay to read about.

To be promotable, the piece must be *timely*—that is, it should be published at a time when the reader is likely to be thinking about the subject or when the reader is most likely to want or need the information in the story. A college football preview, for example, should be published in August or early September, not in October, when the season is already under way; not in February, when the season's over; not in May, before readers are ready to start thinking about football again.

Also to be promotable, the cover story must be *relevant*. It must be newsworthy. It must mean something to the readers. It must be able to satisfactorily answer the question, "Who cares?" A large segment of the magazine's audience must care about the subject and want to know what the cover story can tell them about it.

5. *Illustratability.* The ideal cover story is easily illustratable on the cover with photography or, possibly, compelling artwork. A piece for which photographs cannot be taken and existing photographs are unavailable is handicapped as a potential cover story, forcing the editor to find some other way to present the issue's main piece to readers and potential readers. Those other ways, which include artwork illustration and type-only, often merely make the best of a bad situation and do not permit a truly effective cover.

Illustrating the Cover

The cover illustration is important enough to warrant special attention. Magazine editors naturally have different ideas about how to illustrate the cover. Many of those ideas stem from the editor's own preferences, some from research on single-copy sales, some from the traditions of the magazine. So what works, or what works best, is open to discussion among editors. However, there are some generalizations about cover illustrations that can be made:

■ Photographs usually work better than artwork. For an example, see the cover of *Arizona Highways* (Figure 14.2) and compare it to the *Orange & Blue* cover (Figure 14.1).

■ A photo of a person or a photo that includes a person, or people, works better than a photo without people. Figures 14.3 and 14.4 provide an example from the covers of *Mississippi.*

■ A photo of something specific works better than a photo of something in general. A shot of a person or people in a boat on a picturesque section of the River Shannon, for example, works better than an aerial view of the river.

■ A photo (or artwork) that shows a person in relationship with someone or something pertaining to the story works better than a photo that shows only a person. In many cases, what works in the display inside the magazine is also what works best for the cover illustration. An environmental portrait, for example, that shows the person juxtaposed with whatever it is that makes him or her newsworthy usually works better than a portrait of the person alone.

Figure 14.2.   Reprinted by permission from *Arizona Highways* and with the permission of artist Gary Bennett.

The Importance of Planning

Shooting photos for the cover or painting a cover illustration is not something to be left to chance or the judgment of the photographer or artist. There are cover elements that have to be accommodated by the

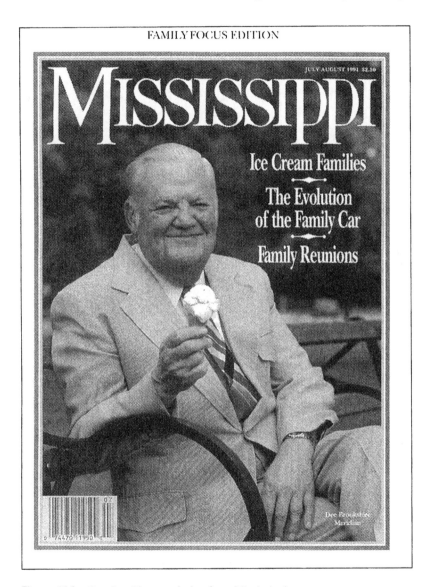

Figure 14.3.   Reprinted by permission from *Mississippi.*

illustration, and so covers have to be composed, more or less, before the photographer shoots or the artist paints.

The magazine's logo, for example, has to appear on the cover, as do the issue date and cover price, and so the cover illustration has to make room for those three elements. If an existing photograph is to be used on the cover, the shot selected will have a light or dark area at the top of the

Figure 14.4.   Reprinted by permission from *Mississippi.*

photograph, where the logo, issue date and cover price (if any) can be superimposed or dropped out. If a photographer is assigned to shoot the cover photo, he or she must be told to shoot with the logo in mind. Unless the magazine runs its logo above the cover illustration on a solid band or a wide border, all photographs shot for the cover *must* have a more or less uniformly dark or uniformly light area at the top of the photograph to allow the superimposition or the reverse of the logo and other type. Don't assume that the photographer knows that and will automatically give you what you need. Tell him, or her; be tactful but explicit. The same need, of course, applies to artwork commissioned for the cover.

In addition to space for the logo, issue date and cover price, the cover illustration must also accommodate cover lines. The photographer must compose the cover photo so there is room to superimpose or drop out the type of the cover lines. When photos are shot without regard for cover lines, it's the editor who ends up with the problem. She has to figure out a way to run cover lines over a variegated background, where type goes from dark to light and back again, causing a severe legibility problem for readers and producing a visual hodgepodge.

There are ways to solve the problem, of course, in case the editor is left without a satisfactory choice of cover photographs. One solution is to mortise a box out of the photo, then fill the mortise with color and overprint the color or reverse the type of the cover lines (Figure 14.5). Another solution is to create a band or ribbon of color or white, then overprint or reverse the cover line in the band or ribbon.

The best way to *avoid* the problem is to tell the photographer or artist to compose the photo or artwork so there is ample room for cover lines.

Cover lines have traditionally been placed down the left side of the cover to accommodate the newsstand practice of overlapping magazines in the racks, with only their left side visible to the browsing buyer. However, supermarkets, drugstores and other single-copy sales outlets have changed their display practices, and many magazines now are displayed either flat with their entire cover visible or standing in the rack, with the top half of the cover visible. For that and other reasons, many magazines, including those sold on newsstands, now place cover lines practically anywhere—down the left side, down the right side, across the bottom, across the top, right top, left top.

So the photographer need not be limited to the left side for the accommodation of cover lines. According to the preference of the editor or art director, space can be provided elsewhere on the cover. That's the good news for the photographer. The bad news is that with greater flexibility on the placement of cover lines, the editor may choose to place them on the left side *and* the right side—and elsewhere, too.

Figure 14.5. Reprinted by permission from *Orange & Blue Magazine.*

In any case, the editor or the magazine's art director or photo editor must visualize not just the cover illustration but the entire cover when the cover photograph or artwork is assigned. And the photographer needs to be told what the cover plan is, so he or she can shoot the cover photo according to the plan.

CHAPTER 15

Cover Lines

The editor who wants a lively, effective cover must master the art of creating cover lines (sometimes called "sell lines" or "cover blurbs"), those promotional headlines that tell the reader what lies beyond the cover. Although part of the cover, which was treated in the previous chapter, cover lines are so important and the writing of them is so special that they warrant a chapter of their own, rather than having to share a chapter with the other cover elements.

Purposes of Cover Lines

For the magazine's subscribers (or those who receive the magazine free), cover lines have a single purpose: Provoke or entice the reader to open the magazine and go inside. For newsstand buyers of the magazine, cover lines have the additional purpose of prompting browsers to buy the magazine. In every case, whether the cover is being seen by a subscriber, by some other recipient of the magazine, by a potential single-copy buyer or by a pass-along reader, cover lines are there to make the magazine more inviting, more appealing, more exciting, more interesting.

It is the inviting, appealing, exciting, interesting magazine that gets read, and getting read is the whole editorial idea of a magazine. The editor cannot assume the magazine will be read simply because it has been placed in the hands or under the eyes of the reader. To compete successfully with other attractions that are seeking the reader's time and attention, a magazine—*every* magazine—must woo and win the reader. Each issue must sell itself to readers or potential readers, and the fundamental purpose of cover lines is to promote that sale.

The Great Cover Line Controversy

Not all magazine editors agree on the importance or even the desirability of cover lines. Some editors think that cover lines sully the cover. They believe the cover should be no more than a pretty picture, like calendar art, a pristine objet d'art that graces the coffee table or nightstand upon which it is displayed like an art book. Other editors make some concession to the need for an explanation of the cover illustration by running an inconspicuous clue, like a caption, on the cover, but otherwise avoid cover lines.

Editors who prefer quiet, pristine covers to those with cover lines tend to hold and, when challenged, defend their preference with passion, devout in their belief that a pretty picture alone will attract readers to the magazine merely because it is a pretty picture. They tend to think of cover lines as tasteless, deleterious to the attractiveness of the cover illustration and altogether wrong for the image of their magazines. What's really wrong, however, is their idea that a picture alone will attract readers to the magazine more effectively than a picture *and* cover lines. The contrast of *Audubon* magazine's covers of the 1980s with those of the 1990s makes the point that covers with cover lines are livelier, more compelling and more effective (Figures 15.1 and 15.2).

Additional evidence that cover lines make for a livelier, more effective cover comes from editors of trade magazines that run cover lines even though their magazines are not sold on the newsstand. Editors of those magazines know that it's not enough to put the magazines in the hands or in the mailboxes of their recipients; they realize that magazines have to *sell* themselves to their intended readers and that they do so by using cover lines to sell the content.

In some cases editors who maintain a hold on the pretty-picture idea of a cover have found a way to have their pristine cover and get cover lines, too. For newsstand sales they wrap a half-cover over the pretty-picture cover, like a flap, with cover lines running down it and a bar code for automated cash registers at the bottom.

Figure 15.1.   Reprinted by permission from *Audubon*.

Kinds of Cover Lines

Cover lines come in three basic varieties:

1. Label. These are the ones that usually contain no verb and make no specific statement to the reader. Here are some examples:

Figure 15.2.   Reprinted by permission from *Audubon.*

OUR VANISHING FORESTS
NEW BREAST CANCER CURES
A GUIDE TO BLOW-OFF COURSES
THE REAL INDIANA JONESES
CHICKEN-FOR-DINNER COOKBOOK

2. *Statement.* This kind of cover line tells the reader something specific. It makes a statement. Here are some examples:

10 WAYS TO BEAT THE TAX HIKE!
WHAT LENO THINKS OF LETTERMAN
HOW TO FIGHT FAT 25 WAYS
SOLAR COOKERS: THEY WORK!
CLINTON'S DOCTOR TELLS WHY BILL RUNS

3. *Question.* These cover lines ask the reader a question, such as:

DOES STANLEY KAPLAN MAKE A DIFFERENCE?
SHOULD YOUR BUSINESS MOVE TO THE EDGE OF TOWN?
WHERE ARE THE BEST PLACES TO LIVE?
BLONDES: DO THEY REALLY HAVE MORE FUN?
HOMOSEXUALS: BORN OR MADE?

Any of the three kinds can be effective, depending on the subject and angle of the piece being promoted by the cover line. In general, however, question cover lines work best when the editor wants to *avoid* making a statement. One good reason to avoid making a statement is that it will give away the story, as in:

NEW SURVEY SHOWS BLONDES
DON'T REALLY HAVE MORE FUN

The idea of a cover line is to drive the reader or potential reader into the magazine and into the piece. A question cover line is intended to urge the reader to read the piece and discover the answer to the question for herself. If the cover line provides the answer, there is not so much incentive for the reader to go inside the magazine and read the piece itself.

Another reason to avoid making a statement is that the editor does not wish to make a controversial assertion or draw a conclusion about a controversial subject. For example, if a cover line reads

THE MAN WILL ROGERS NEVER MET

the magazine makes an editorial statement. It expresses the opinion of its owner, publisher or editor that the subject of the article is so unlikable that even Will Rogers, the man who said he never met a man he didn't like, wouldn't like him. But if the cover line reads

IS HE THE MAN WILL ROGERS NEVER MET?

a conclusion is unexpressed and the reader must draw it for himself/herself after reading the piece.

Effective Cover Lines: How to Write Them

The starting place for effective cover lines is the pieces that the cover lines are intended to promote. For cover lines to be effective they must refer to pieces that are promotable, that are the most promotable pieces in the issue. The pieces must be interesting, important, provocative, relevant or possess some other compelling quality. Once the editor has decided which pieces are the most promotable, he or she is ready to apply the rules of writing effective cover lines.

Rule 1: Go Straight to the Angle

Every piece chosen for cover lines should have a clear angle, which ordinarily provides the cover line's message. If the angle, or idea, of the article is "Do blondes really have more fun?" and the piece is a survey—with anecdotes and lively quotes—of women who have changed their hair color and become blondes, the cover line should go straight to the heart of the piece:

DO BLONDES REALLY HAVE MORE FUN?

Or:

DO BLONDES REALLY
HAVE MORE FUN?—
A New Survey's
Surprising Results

The editor, or whoever is to write the cover lines, must be totally familiar with the pieces that are to get cover lines. Rereading the pieces is the best way to make sure you and your cover-line writer see the angles clearly.

Rule 2: Pick What Is Most Interesting

Realistically speaking, there will be times when the angle is not all that clear, times when an article has no one main message but several interesting or worthwhile messages instead. An "interview with" piece, for example, particularly a Q&A, probably won't have a central idea around which the article is built, but the piece will touch on a number of relevant, provocative topics.

When that happens, remember there's a significant difference between cover lines and titles. Titles ought to go to the heart of the piece, to capture its message or mood, to represent the total piece. Cover lines, on the other hand, are more like advertisements; they don't have to talk about the whole article, but can focus on one aspect of the piece instead. A Q&A piece on U.S. Supreme Court Justice Ruth Bader Ginsburg, for example, might cover a wide range of topics—from her childhood experiences to her days in law school to her experiences as an attorney in women's causes to service on the U.S. Court of Appeals to her marriage, her family, her home life, her dealings with President Bill Clinton, her first six months on the Supreme Court and so on. The cover line, however, may pick one of those topics to play up. It might read like this:

JUSTICE GINSBURG'S
DISCOVERIES ON THE
U.S. SUPREME COURT

Or like this:

JUSTICE GINSBURG TALKS
ABOUT LIFE ON SUPREME COURT

Or this:

JUSTICE GINSBURG VIEWS
HER FIRST 180 DAYS ON
THE U.S. SUPREME COURT

Or:

The First 180 Days as a Supreme Court Justice:
AN EXCLUSIVE INTERVIEW WITH RUTH BADER
GINSBURG

Are those cover lines misleading? Not if the article gives the reader the information promised in the cover lines. The Ginsburg piece includes other material, granted, but from the editor's perspective, it especially includes the material emphasized in the cover line. The editor, recognizing that the cover is intended to sell the magazine by selling its content, is simply showing the best side of this particular piece of content. That's what the editor—and the cover lines—are supposed to do.

Rule 3. Specific Is Better than Vague

Specific is always better, even when the specific covers only a small part of the story while the vague covers the whole piece. In the case of the hypothetical Ginsburg Q&A article, for example, a cover line that says

JUSTICE GINSBURG VIEWS
HER FIRST 180 DAYS ON
THE U.S. SUPREME COURT

is more provocative than a cover line that reads

A Q&A WITH JUSTICE RUTH BADER GINSBURG

or one that .reads

AN INTERVIEW WITH
RUTH BADER GINSBURG

Tell the reader something specific, but make sure it is an *interesting* something.

Also, cover lines for how-to pieces are usually better when the "how to" is in the cover line. The inclusion of the words "how to" makes the cover line more specific.

HOW TO DEAL WITH A DIFFICULT BOSS

for example, is better than

DEALING WITH A DIFFICULT BOSS

and

HOW TO PROTECT YOURSELF FROM STALKERS

is better than

PROTECT YOURSELF FROM STALKERS

Rule 4: Keep It Concise

The idea is to say it quickly because you want the reader to be able to read it quickly. Say it in as few words as possible, but use enough words to say what must be said. The trick is to avoid all *unnecessary* words. Sometimes it is enough to give the reader an impression, without taking a lot of words to say it as a sentence, as in these cover lines from *Lear's*:

FATAL APPLIANCES
The Current Scare

JEAN HARRIS
on Crimes of Fashion

It's possible for a cover line to be *too* concise. When it is, vagueness results, as it does with these four cover lines, all of which appeared on the same cover:

CHARROS
NAVAJO FAIR
MOUNTAIN HIKE
FIESTA WEAR

Those cover lines need more words to make them more explicit, to create a clearer impression in the reader's mind, to more effectively arouse interest.

Rule 5: Make It Perfectly Clear

Here's where the dilettantes and other amateurs get separated from the professionals. *Real* editors should know what cover lines are for. They should know that cover lines must convey a clear message to the reader or potential reader of the magazine. Real editors shouldn't fool around, trying to be cute or overly clever with cover lines and sacrificing explicitness for wit, effectiveness for effect. An example, from a car magazine:

PLAYING CHECKERS IN N.Y.C.

When the reader eventually reaches the piece in the magazine, he discovers that the cover line is a misleading pun that refers to an article about fans and collectors of Checker automobiles. Another example, from the same car magazine:

NEW SAAB 900
KEY DECISION
It's still on the floor, but what's underneath is all new

If the reader gets around to reading the article, he learns that in Saabs the ignition switch is on the floorboard; he also learns that Saab is introducing a new car, the 900, and it, too, has the ignition switch on the floor. The cover line is a senseless pun, leapfrogging from ignition switch on the floor to key to "key decision." To readers, it's a riddle. (Even if the meaning were clear, why would the cover-line writer focus on the placement of the ignition switch when there's so much else to point out? Baffling.)

Another killer of clarity is the inside-out cover line, similar to the inside-out title described in Chapter 7. Like the title with the same problem, the inside-out cover line makes no sense until the reader reads the story. A couple of examples:

TORNADO DOWN!
GENE HACKMAN'S WINNING WAVE

If the reader wishes to investigate, even though there's little incentive to do so, she will find upon turning to the article that the "tornado" in the cover line is not a tornado. It is a British airplane. And "Tornado

Down" is the title of a book about two fliers shot down in Iraq. As for the meaning of "Gene Hackman's winning wave," it's hard to imagine anyone but a serious Gene Hackman fan being curious enough to seek it.

The point is, if the cover line does not send a clear message to the reader, it might as well be printed in the language of the Klingons. Readers won't understand that either.

Rule 6: Long Isn't Always Bad

In some cases additional words can make cover lines more provocative, more enticing. An example from *Good Housekeeping*:

LONI
ANDERSON
TALKS ABOUT
HER DIVORCE
FROM
BURT REYNOLDS
"The night
before,
Burt told
me I was
the love
of his
life. ...
The next
morning I
was served
with divorce
papers ..."

Length does not necessarily defeat conciseness. Cover lines should be concise, without unnecessary words, but when more words give more appeal to the cover line, use them.

Rule 7: Arrest and Arouse

Cover lines are supposed to stop the browser's roving eye and ignite curiosity. Effective cover lines cannot be bland or say-nothing, like these from a home-and-garden magazine:

DECORATING TODAY
THE PROFESSION'S RISING STARS

Or these from a gardening magazine:

SUMMER GLORIES
PERENNIAL PLEASURES

Or these from a city magazine:

GET READY FOR THE ULTIMATE JOURNEY
EVENTS GALORE!

Or these from a regional magazine:

A SOUTHERN LITERARY JOURNEY

DECORATING
Personal Style With
A Professional
Touch

The moral: Make the cover lines speak up and say something interesting and interest-arousing. Remember that cover lines are there to animate, not decorate, the cover.

Rule 8: There's No Business without Show Business

To create effective cover lines, the editor must not be averse to some hype, a bit of show biz. All communication media, particularly mass media, do their jobs better when they use a little show business, doing certain things, saying certain things, saying them in a certain way—in order to command and hold the interest of their intended audience more effectively, more successfully. Magazine readers—no matter the kind of magazine—are subject to the same interest-arousing, interest-holding phenomena that affect practically all other healthy-minded humans.

When applied to cover lines, those phenomena dictate the use of certain words that, merely by their inclusion, cause heightened interest among readers. Here are some of them:

new
surprising
exclusive
special
intimate
personal
reveals
you
your

For example, a cover line that promotes an article about college students and their religious faith could read:

RELIGION ON THE CAMPUS

That's not bad, but it's a little quiet. Look what happens when a bit of show-biz is added:

A SPECIAL REPORT:
RELIGION ON THE CAMPUS

The addition of "a special report" makes the piece seem more urgent, more—well, *special*. Now look at a cover line promoting a Q&A with Justice Ruth Bader Ginsburg:

AN INTERVIEW WITH
JUSTICE RUTH GINSBURG

It's adequate. But it can be improved by adding a few show-biz words:

IN THIS ISSUE:
An Exclusive Interview with
JUSTICE RUTH GINSBURG

What more do the additional words actually say? Nothing, really. But they make the piece seem more important, more—special. Another example:

HOW TO BUILD
A SUMMER OASIS

It's okay, but can be made slightly better:

HOW TO BUILD YOUR
OWN SUMMER OASIS

The show-biz words warm it up and make it more personal for the reader.

There's hardly a business alive today that doesn't use some hype and show-biz language to promote its product or service. Magazines, commercial and otherwise, need to do the same. Cover lines are an appropriate place to do it.

Rule 9: Start with the Title

Generally, the best place to begin the search for a cover line is the title of the piece, especially if the title is straightforward, clearly saying what the piece is about. Here are some examples of straightforward titles from *Reader's Digest*:

HOW THE CREDIT CARD CAPTURED AMERICA
CAN YOU TRUST YOUR DOCTOR?
HOW TO HANDLE A HOSTILE DRIVER
EASY WAYS TO PROTECT YOUR HOME
THIS TOWN FIRED ITS GOVERNMENT
WHAT EVERY WOMAN NEEDS TO KNOW ABOUT ESTROGEN
SHE WROTE AMERICA'S FAVORITE SONG

Some of those titles can be used verbatim as cover lines; others need minor work to convert them to cover lines. All are clear, concise and, for many readers, relevant.

Throwaway titles and others lacking explicitness can sometimes be adapted to make a cover line, particularly if the information in the subtitle can be worked into the cover line. Here's a throwaway title from *Reader's Digest*:

The Punk and the Tyrant

It's too obscure to make a cover line, but if words are added to it, like a subtitle, it can work. Like this:

THE PUNK AND THE TYRANT:
The Story of Olympic Swimmer
Nelson Diebel and His Coach

Or, with a little show-biz language, it could read this way:

THE PUNK AND THE TYRANT:
The story of an Olympic
winner and a coach mean
enough to challenge him

When there's not enough room on the cover to accommodate all those words—which is the usual situation—the throwaway title is the first piece of excess baggage to be jettisoned. Such mysterious language is okay for the title, near which can be found space for a long, explicit and even show-bizzy subtitle, but for a cover line, that throwaway title is a useless and cumbersome load. It does, however, yield the idea of the piece, and an effective cover line can be written from the idea. Like this:

The Olympic swimmer
whose coach was mean
enough to let him win

Or this:

Olympian Nelson Diebel:
His coach was mean enough
to let him win a gold medal

The wise editor first writes titles and subtitles, or has them written. Then, when it's time to put together the cover, he turns back to the titles to help him create concise, eloquent, effective cover lines.

Rule 10: Get It Down, Then Mess Around

As with title writing, the best way to craft a good cover line is to get down on paper or on your monitor *the idea of the piece*. Once it is captured in words, you can take away words or add them, move them around, smooth them out, line them up the way you want them to appear to the reader. You can write a statement cover line, then edit it down to a label if the statement or the verb isn't necessary. Or you can turn the statement upside down and try it as a question.

When there are two ideas that must be included in the cover line, you can try to say them in one statement or say them separately and connect them with a colon, a dash or some other visual device. For example, a story about the danger of courtship violence, told from the perspective of three victims, could be promoted with a cover line like this:

COURTSHIP VIOLENCE
Victims
Tell
Their
Stories

Or this:

COURTSHIP VIOLENCE:
Victims Tell Their Stories

The creation of effective cover lines is much more likely to occur when the editor, or her designated cover line writer, allows ample time to write them. Sometimes good cover lines spring almost instantaneously from the writer's creative lobe; other times, they take time and an editor's determination to hang in and try again and again until the cover line is precisely right.

One Final Word: Legibility

Many good cover lines have been wasted by poor or uncomprehending art direction. The editor must insist—usually to the art director—that cover lines be easily read. Being easily read means that all conditions for legibility have to be right—type size, type face, background, color.

Some art directors, particularly new ones, fail to understand the importance of cover lines, considering them a defilement of art, like a mustache penciled onto the *Mona Lisa*. The wise editor will be tactfully firm with such an art director, insisting that cover lines be clearly legible, not just up close but from at least six feet away. Insist.

CHAPTER 16

The Production Process

In a sense, the production process has already begun even before the editor starts planning an issue. It is, after all, the deadline set by the printer that determines the editorial department's deadlines for producing the magazine, from the earliest planning meeting to the day that all materials are sent to the printer.

Simply put, the usual first production step is for the magazine's publisher to tell the printer when the magazine is to be put into the mail or delivered to the distributor, or both. The printer then tells the publisher, or the editor, when camera-ready copy must be at the printer's in order to have the issue printed and bound by the date the publisher stipulates. Then the editor, or a designated staff member, draws up the production schedule for the issue.

And so the entire editorial process of producing the materials for the magazine is governed by the production process.

Practically speaking, however, the production process begins when the creative work of writers, editors, photographers, illustrators and art directors is done.

The Basic Steps of Production

Changes in the methods and equipment used to produce magazines continue to occur so rapidly that anything written about the production process runs the risk of being outdated by the time it reaches print.

The most fundamental production steps, however, those that traditionally have been under the editor's close supervision, remain unchanged even though the ways to accomplish them keep changing. To make magazines, today as always, it is still necessary to: (1) set type; (2) compose the pages; and (3) deliver camera-ready copy to the printer.

What has changed, because of electronic technology, is the *how* of those production steps. Type is now, in effect, set by the magazine's writers and editors when they input their copy into their computers. Pages are composed, or paginated, on a computer monitor, the computer having been loaded with one of the several available desktop publishing software systems. Camera-ready copy can be a computer printout that serves as a mechanical, together with the cropped and sized photos and artwork and color separations. Or it might be a floppy disk plus cropped and sized photos and artwork and separations. *Or* it might be a floppy disk with all line art, halftones and color photos and artwork having been scanned into the computer-generated pages.

After those basic production steps comes the work of the printer, whose pre-press methods and equipment have undergone electronic changes to match—to interface with—those occurring in the magazine's editorial offices.

In-House Desktop Publishing Procedures

In today's electronic environment many beginning editors will have learned at least one desktop publishing (DTP) system before getting their first job. On many magazines, in fact, a working knowledge of DTP, sometimes even experience with a particular software system (such as Pagemaker, Ventura or Quark XPress) and particular hardware (such as Macintosh) is either a requirement or an important consideration for employment. In other situations, new editors quickly learn the system in use by their magazines.

For the editor, in-house DTP procedures are mostly a boon. They save time by speeding up typesetting and page composition, thereby shortening the magazine's lead time (the time it takes to produce the finished magazine, from planning to printing). A short lead time is important because it allows the magazine to be more timely, more current. Being able to produce a magazine, from scheduling to arrival on the newsstand, in four weeks, for example, is a lot better than needing eight weeks to do it. The content in that case is four weeks fresher.

In-house DTP also allows the editor tighter control over the production process. Changes and corrections, especially including those necessary at the last minute, can be made instantly, mere steps away from the editor's office, instead of at a typesetting service or printing company perhaps miles away.

Over the long run, in-house DTP also saves the magazine money. It represents the magazine's doing something for itself instead of paying someone else to do it. It is, in effect, an elimination of the middleman.

Changes made by the editorial department after the type has been set or after the page has been composed are called *author's alterations* or *author's revises*, often shortened to *AAs* or *ARs*. Charges from the typesetting service or printer for AAs can be staggering. In-house DTP can effect a substantial savings merely in the cost of AAs, which for many magazines, despite all efforts to reduce their number, remain an unavoidable evil in the production process.

The major problem with in-house DTP is that it turns editors and art directors into typesetters, compositors and paste-up artists, requiring editorial staff members to master production and computer skills and to devote a significant part of their working day to production functions instead of purely editorial functions. Most editors, however, would probably agree that that problem is a small price to pay for the convenience, control, speed and economy afforded by in-house desktop publishing procedures.

Farming It Out

For the magazine that is a going concern, in-house DTP is the state-of-the-art way of putting a magazine together efficiently, speedily and economically. For start-up or small, struggling magazines, however, particularly those published less frequently than once a month, the cost of equipment and software, plus the time required to learn how to use computer, scanner and printer effectively, or teach their use to a bare-bones and already overburdened staff, may be more than an entrepreneuring editor or publisher wants to take on at the moment.

In that case, help can be found elsewhere. Any decent-sized city is now likely to have an array of typesetting businesses that will not only set type but paginate and provide camera-ready copy to you for your printer, using either DTP procedures or phototypesetting and photocomposition.

For best results, the magazine's art director—or whoever is serving in that capacity—provides rough layouts and marked copy to the typesetting service. All copy, including text, titles, subtitles, blurbs, captions, the table of contents—the whole content of the magazine—is "specked." That is, the art director specifies on the copy the type face, type size, leading and line width for each piece of copy, plus any other necessary instructions. Type faces are chosen by the art director from those available at the typesetting service. All copy is keyed to the layouts, to show where the text and each element of display go.

If the magazine has no art director—not even a part-timer or free-lancer—the editor ordinarily can get design help from the typesetting service, for an additional fee.

The editor seeking help from a typesetting service should shop around for the one that will work best. The three big considerations in choosing one service over the others are (1) price, (2) quality and (3) service.

To accurately estimate what it will cost the magazine to have type set and pages made, and to be able to compare prices from various typesetting firms, it's best to have the firms quote a *price per page*, rather than a price per hour. They will want to give you a price per hour, however, and so you must urge them to translate that price into a price per page or price per spread.

Make sure you see some work they have done for other customers, so you can determine if the quality of their work is acceptable for your magazine. Also, it's a good idea to get names of some of their customers, so you can check with them about the firm's service. Does the firm meet the customer's deadlines? How fast can it process a customer's material? Is a sympathetic and responsive ear available when the customer has a problem? Does the firm deliver what it promises?

When you first talk to the typesetting firm's representative, talk to him or her in person *at* the firm's place of business—so you can get an impression of the people you would be dealing with and so you can see if it looks like a fly-by-night operation in a seedy storefront or a half-baked operation in somebody's garage, or a substantial, stable and reputable business run by competent professionals.

Proofing

Careful and repeated proofreading is the surest way to eliminate typographical and other errors that, for all the editors' diligence, have a terrible tendency to lie hidden until the magazine has been printed and then glow from the page like lighted neon.

All copy—text, titles, everything—should be carefully proofread after it is input into the computer. It should be proofed again after pagination and proofed again before camera-ready copy is sent to the printer.

Once the materials are delivered to the printer, problems become more complicated and more costly to solve. Ordinarily the printer will provide the editor with a proof of the entire issue—usually called bluelines, which are photographic prints of the pages of the magazine, trimmed and bound to simulate the magazine itself. Bluelines, however, are not meant to let editors discover 10-point typos—or any other kind. They are to let the editor see that the printer has correctly placed all artwork and photographs and correctly assembled all the pages in the issue. Errors uncaught until the editor sees the printer's bluelines will require resetting type, remaking camera-ready copy and reshooting the film from which the press plates are made—resulting in delays and in additional, expensive and unnecessary costs. The only alternative then is to let the typos run, which is not what a conscientious editor wants to do.

The prudent editor will remember that meticulous proofing is to the production of a magazine what preventive maintenance is to the operation of an automobile: It keeps things from going wrong and avoids big repair bills.

How to Live Happily with a Printer

Printers can be difficult to get along with. Like a charming but unfaithful spouse, a printer, particularly when he's courting your business, can make many glib promises that later he will break without disturbing his conscience or owning up to his perfidy.

To the editorial staff he can be arrogant, condescending, aloof, duplicitous, irresponsible and unreliable. He may treat you like a dummy or an annoyance. When things go wrong, he may accuse you, or someone on your staff, of creating the problem. Some printers will adroitly play the editorial department against the publisher, who pays their bill, so that the blame for anything to which the publisher objects is laid on the desks of the editorial department, for which you are directly responsible, and thus the failing becomes yours.

It is possible, of course, to have a printer you love and live happily with. Here are a few fundamental rules for achieving happiness with a printer.

Rule 1: Choose Well

As in marriage, a good relationship doesn't come from a bad choice. And so the prudent editor will select a printer wisely and carefully if he or she is to be happy with the choice. The criteria to be applied to a prospective printer are the same as those used in selecting a typesetting service:

■ *Price.* What you would really like is the dream printer—one who will do everything right and on time, be a delight to work with, give you good advice, help you avoid mistakes and make you look good by making the magazine look wonderful. It's a whole lot easier to find such a printer if your magazine has money to burn and doesn't mind a whopping production budget. Few are like that, however.

For most magazines the trick is to find the right printer at the right price. Cost will always be a consideration, and so the prudent editor and publisher will determine how much the magazine can afford and set out to find the printer who will give the most for the money.

■ *Quality.* No editor wants schlock—which may result naturally from a rock-bottom, no-frills printing price or may be caused by the printer's incompetence and/or lack of appropriate equipment. The wise editor will make sure he or she sees a prospective printer's work before entrusting the magazine to him. You should ask for samples of his work, other magazines that the printer prints. Be satisfied that the printer you're considering can give you the result you want.

Be wary of the printer who can't show you other magazines he has printed because his business is now limited to brochures, flyers and mailing pieces or black-and-white newsprint tabloids. He's looking at your account as his break into magazine printing. He very likely will be learning on the job—your job—and you may end up giving him more help than he gives you.

■ *Service.* You should satisfy yourself that the prospective printer meets deadlines, delivers when he is supposed to, returns phone calls promptly, listens attentively to questions, gives accurate and helpful answers, is pleasant to deal with and generally treats you and your staff members in a way that indicates he appreciates your magazine's business.

To find out how he treats customers and how he runs his business, ask him for the names and phone numbers of some of his customers, then give them a call and hear what they have to say.

Ordinarily, it's a good idea for a small magazine, one with a relatively short press run, to pick a small printing company or one that specializes in short-run publications. A big magazine, one with a press run in the hundreds of thousands, or more, will probably require a big printer, one with enough equipment, space and experience to handle a run of that size. A small magazine at a big printer is likely to get second-class treatment while the printer's big accounts get preferential treatment when schedules conflict or emergencies arise.

One thing that is not terribly important in picking a printer is proximity. A printer can be anywhere in the country and still be able to receive or send materials overnight, so that they reach either the printer or the editorial department no later than the next day, or even the next morning. Magazines going to subscribers can be placed into the mail from any location in the country, and those going to the newsstand distributor or elsewhere can be trucked to their destination, usually overnight if the printer is within 600 or so miles. Freight charges, of course, must be added in when the cost of printing is being considered.

Rule 2: Assert Your Influence

The magazine's publisher may be the person who makes the ultimate decision on a printer, but the wise editor will realize that it is to the editor's—and the magazine's—advantage to have the publisher include the editor in the selection process. If the selection is the publisher's decision and the publisher doesn't think of it first, the editor should tactfully suggest that the editor or the managing editor (if there is one) and probably the art director be included in the selection process, long before a decision is made. It's important for the printer to see that the editorial department has a say in the decision-making and that while he is answerable to the publisher, who pays the bills, he will be accountable also to the editorial department generally and to the editor in particular.

Rule 3: See the Invoices Before They're Paid

If it's the publisher who pays the printer's bill, he or she may be paying more than legitimate costs when there are extra charges on the invoice. That possibility is especially present when the printer charges the magazine for author's alterations. To help make the printer more accountable to the editorial department, to make sure the magazine does not overpay and to prevent the magazine's publisher or owner from unjustly blaming the editorial department—and thus the editor—for increased production costs, you should tactfully insist on seeing the printer's bill before it is paid. If there are extra charges listed, carefully check them. (If they are legitimate, you may want to talk to your staff again about the importance of keeping AAs to an absolute minimum and production costs generally under control.) If they are not legitimate, tell the publisher and be ready to work out a revised invoice with the printer.

Rule 4: Don't Sign a Contract if You Can Avoid It

Contracts between the magazine and the printer are mostly, if not entirely, to the benefit of the printer. The editor's ultimate power with the printer is his or her freedom to move the magazine to another printer if quality or service degenerates or cost rises. A contract can prevent a rise in printing cost during the term of the contract, but it does nothing to prevent service or quality from deteriorating.

A short-run magazine, which does not require a huge quantity of paper to be bought in advance by the printer, as large magazines may require, should not need a printer's contract, binding the publisher and the editor to the printer for multiple issues. Get a firm price from the printer, which binds him, but don't sign a contract, which binds the magazine.

The Last Word

To the printer belongs the ultimate task of producing the magazine, turning the creation of the staff and freelancers into printed pages. The results and the relationship are so important that they are well worth the editor's best efforts to pick and keep a printer with whom the editor can work happily and satisfyingly.

CHAPTER 17

Legal Bugaboos and Journalistic Ethics

A lthough most editors spend an entire career without facing even the threat of a lawsuit, all editors need to know how to avoid potential litigation concerning the material they publish. And when the potential for litigation is unavoidable, as it sometimes is, the editor needs to know how to proceed.

Editing a magazine without knowledge of the legal responsibilities and hazards of publishing is like driving a car blindfolded; you can run into all sorts of trouble if you do it. What is said in this chapter, however, is not and isn't intended to be guidance sufficient to cover every potentially litigious situation or the fine points of *any* such situation. It is intended merely to caution beginning editors and give them enough knowledge to recognize the red flags of warning.

The editor is especially concerned with three areas of the law:

Libel

Libel is a printed or written statement that is (1) false and (2) defamatory. It is something untrue that your magazine publishes about a person, causing that person to suffer public hatred, contempt or ridicule or injury to his or her business or occupation—or, in some instances, simply making those consequences likely.

A libel case is usually a civil action brought in a state court, under state laws, which vary from state to state. It might also be a criminal action, prosecuted by the state, which is rare.

A successful libel suit can result in penalties not only against your magazine's owner but against you as the editor and possibly other members of the magazine's staff as well as the author of the offending piece. It can damage the reputation and injure the profitability of the magazine. Even if the libel suit is unsuccessful, it can cost your magazine a bundle of money to defend. It can also play havoc with your career. It is the chief legal bugaboo for every editor and every publication. It is the ultimate editorial horror.

Publications can use one or more of several possible defenses against a libel suit, depending on the circumstances in reporting and writing the offending story and also depending on whether the person claiming libel is a public official or a public figure or a *private* figure.

Public officials (such as government officials) and public figures (such as celebrities of various kinds), in order to prevail in a libel suit, must prove malice on the part of the publication's editors. "Malice" in such cases means that the publication's editors knew the information was false or had serious doubts about its truth—but published it anyway.

For a private figure (which is everyone who is neither a public official nor a public figure), proving malice isn't necessary. A private figure needs only to show that the publication's editors were negligent or reckless in publishing the libelous material. The publication's editors could be considered negligent if they failed to research the story adequately and thus failed to discover, as they should have, that the information was false. The editors could be considered reckless if they published the material without regard for its truth or falsity. Any time an editor spots in a story a statement that defames or tends to defame someone, even a notorious character, a Klaxon should go off in the editor's head. It doesn't matter whether the statement is in the words of the author or in a quote from the author's source; if it might damage someone's reputation or lower the esteem in which that person is held in the community or among his friends, or if it might hurt him in his job or his business, that statement must be regarded as potentially libelous. Furthermore, the person who might be injured by the statement need not be named in the story. If he or she can be otherwise identified—by context or by job or address or physical description or in any other way—the potential for libel still exists.

Editors must be especially watchful for potentially libelous statements in an investigative article and any other piece that deals with a controversy.

The editor's best defense against a libel suit is to avoid it. The surest way to avoid it is to delete potentially libelous material from the story. Just take it out.

The second best defense, to be used when the defamatory material must stay in the story, is to be able to *prove that it is true*.

The editor must remember that it is not enough for the defamatory statement to *be* true; it must be *provably* true. That is, you must have proof that will convince a jury that the statement is true.

When you're beginning to think of running a piece that includes defamatory material, it's time to talk to the magazine's house lawyer and show him (or her) the story and what you have as proof of its accuracy. If your magazine does not have a house lawyer or an attorney it uses regularly, find an attorney whose practice includes communications law. If you don't know one, ask the local bar association to give you names. Let the attorney advise you on the adequacy of the proof and tell you if more is needed or if the story may be edited to accommodate the proof that you do have. His advice is very likely to be: (a) go with what you've got; or (b) get more proof; or (c) alter the story; or (d) kill it. Make your decision after hearing the expert's advice.

A person who has consented to the publication of defamatory material about himself ordinarily cannot later claim libel. Therefore, one other way the magazine's editor may protect the magazine and its workers from a libel suit is to be able to prove that the offended person consented to the publication of the material. And so when the editor sees potentially libelous material in a piece, two of the first questions to ask are, "Was there consent?" and, "Can we prove consent?" If the answer to either question is "no," the safest move is to delete the material from the story. If it's not crucial to the story, there's probably no good reason for leaving it in.

Another defense against libel is that the defamatory statement is not presented to readers as a fact but is the opinion or fair comment of the writer. The editor of a magazine that runs reviews, columns, editorials or features such as best-and-worst pieces needs to be wary about the statement that makes an opinion look like a fact and he should edit the piece accordingly. To further help avoid the potential for libel, the editor should insist that the writer give not just his or her opinion but reasons, at least one, for the opinion. The editor must also make sure that the object of criticism is of interest to the public, not merely to the writer.

In every piece, the editor needs to be alert to the possibility of libel if there is any statement or quote or purported fact that has the potential to defame. The prudent editor therefore will read every piece in manuscript form before it is scheduled into the magazine and read it again after it has been edited and is in page form. Second best is designating a trusted, trustworthy staff member to read the pieces when the editor can't.

Invasion of Privacy

Here is the other big legal bugaboo of print media. Fortunately, magazines are not as likely to commit the offense as are daily newspapers, the writers and editors of which are often forced to work with unwilling or reluctant sources and under the intense pressure of short deadlines.

In the United States, people have a right to privacy—a right to be let alone, to be free from unwarranted publicity. An invasion of privacy is an infringement of that right.

An article on AIDS that tells an anecdote about a victim of the disease, naming him and describing the present circumstances of his life, even though all the details are provably true and therefore not libelous, may result in a lawsuit against the magazine and its editor and the author of the article. If the AIDS victim's homosexual companion is also named or otherwise identified in the article, the magazine and its workers may face an invasion of privacy suit by the companion as well as the victim.

A profile of a bar bouncer that is illustrated on its opening page by a posed shot of the bouncer inside the bar might result in an invasion of privacy suit if one or more of the bar's patrons, seen seated at the bar behind the bouncer, is identifiable in the photograph.

As with libel, the best defense against invasion of privacy is avoidance. Having the AIDS victim give his consent to being identified and having his story told will head off a lawsuit by him. His companion's consent will likewise avoid a lawsuit by him. If the companion won't give consent, delete his name and other identifying information from the story.

If the AIDS victim refuses consent, cut him out of the article and replace him with someone who is more cooperative. Or if his material is so good that you feel you must have it in the piece, but he won't let you identify him, offer to use a pseudonym for him and to otherwise cloud his identity. If he won't go for that either, dump him—no matter how good the material is—and get somebody else.

In actual practice, however, when a magazine writer identifies himself as a writer and tells the source what he wants and the source consents to an interview, the source is also consenting to publication of the material he gives the writer during the interview. That consent may not be according to the law, but it is certainly according to normal human behavior. Sources—private figures or otherwise—who don't want to provide the information and don't want it published will simply decline the writer's request for an interview. Or else they will grant the interview but decline to answer objectionable questions or simply will not talk about subjects they consider none of the writer's or public's business.

In those cases, the magazine's writer will immediately discover the parts of the story to which the source is *not* consenting, and ordinarily the editor or the assigning editor will soon learn about them from the writer.

If the source is a private figure, the editor's best move is to back off—either from the whole story or from the parts of it the source doesn't want to talk about.

If the source is a public official or a public figure, consent may not be necessary. The magazine's writer might obtain the desired information from other sources and use it despite the objections of the public official or public figure. In such cases, the person's newsworthiness as a public official or public figure may, to some extent, deprive him of his right to privacy. However, the lives of even the most public of officials or figures have certain inviolable areas of privacy, and a magazine's trespass into those areas can result in a successful invasion of privacy lawsuit.

To avoid invading the privacy of identifiable bar patrons in the background of the bouncer portrait, the editor (and art director or photo editor and photographer) have several choices. One is to have the people at the bar, and others who are likely to appear in the photo, give their consent and sign releases stating that they have consented. Another is to use models instead of actual patrons at the bar, shooting the photographs before the bar opens or after it closes. Another, of course, is to avoid background people altogether and do the shoot before the bar opens or after it closes, with the barstools empty. Whatever is necessary to avoid the possibility of invasion of privacy in such situations, do—and make sure the photographer is aware of the potential problem.

There is one other practical matter of concern involving privacy. It is the sort of invasion of privacy that's called "intrusion." In cases of intrusion, it doesn't matter whether the magazine has published something objectionable. Merely *acquiring* the material is an invasion of privacy.

Intrusion occurs when reporters or writers force themselves onto the sources, either intruding by trespassing on private property or intruding with a recorder or a listening device or a camera. A writer or photographer who misrepresents himself to gain access to the source may be guilty of intrusion, and intrusion can also result from a writer's use of a recorder to tape a telephone conversation without the source's permission.

The prudent editor will caution writers, particularly those working on investigative pieces, that they should do nothing to expose the magazine or themselves to a possible invasion of privacy lawsuit.

Copyright

Although it's not a bugaboo, copyright is another area of the law that the editor must know about. It applies to magazines in two ways: (1) It protects the magazine's rights to its material; and (2) it prohibits the magazine's unauthorized use of material belonging to others.

To make sure its content is protected under the copyright law, the magazine will have each issue copyrighted, which is easily done by paying a relatively small fee and completing a form obtainable from the U.S. Copyright Office, Library of Congress, Washington, D.C. 20559.

The wise editor will also make certain that the magazine does indeed own the material it pays for and publishes (except, of course, for excerpts or reprinted articles). When it buys a piece from a freelance writer, the magazine should buy *all rights*. Buying all rights makes it a lot simpler to reuse the material in reprints, anthologies, promotional material or any other way the magazine or its publisher later decides, including reprinting for a fee or free in some other magazine.

Every piece done by a freelancer, as well as each piece written by a staff member, should be what the Copyright Office calls a *work made for hire*. That is, the piece is written by an employee in the scope of his or her job, or the piece is commissioned by the magazine and is written by a freelancer. Payment for a freelance piece should be made conditional on the freelancer's agreement that it is a work made for hire. The way to accomplish that agreement is to tell the author at the outset of the assignment that it is to be a work made for hire, then send him or her a written reminder and, finally, write or stamp on the back of the payment check a statement that says that the freelancer, by endorsing the check, is acknowledging that the piece he or she is being paid for is a work made for hire. For copyright purposes then, the magazine is considered the author of the piece.

The magazine should also buy all rights to photographs and artwork illustration that it assigns. In some cases rights can be negotiated at the time the photo assignment is made. The editor would expect to pay less than the photographer's going rate if the magazine bought less than full rights.

Quoted Material

In general, material copyrighted by someone else may be quoted without the author's permission and without violating the copyright *if* the quoted passage is not substantial. A sentence, or even several sentences, wouldn't be considered substantial. Several hundred words, however, might be. In cases where the piece you intend to publish includes more than about 200 words from something previously published, the safest way to proceed is to get permission to use the material.

Such quoted material should also be credited. The reader should be told where those words came from. Particularly if the quote is substantial and its source is not credited, the magazine and the piece's author may be guilty of another offense—*plagiarism*, which is the act of passing off another's work as your own.

The editor needs to know, however, that facts cannot be copyrighted and cannot be plagiarized. It is the way the facts are stated, the combination of words that contain the facts, that is protected by law.

Recommended Additional Reading

Editors who would like to know more about libel law may find more detailed information in the following books and booklets: *The Practical Guide to Libel Law*, by Neil J. Rosini; *The Law of Public Communication*, by Kent R. Middleton and Bill F. Chamberlin; *The Associated Press Stylebook and Libel Manual*; *Synopsis of the Law of Libel and the Right of Privacy*, by Bruce W. Sanford.

For additional information on invasion of privacy, editors may consult Middleton and Chamberlin's *The Law of Public Communication,* Sanford's *Synopsis of the Law of Libel and the Right of Privacy* and *The Associated Press Stylebook and Libel Manual.*

Information about the U.S. copyright law and copyright procedures may be obtained from the Copyright Office (see address above).

Ethics and Professional Practices

In addition to the legal considerations, there are ethical aspects of managing a magazine that every editor should know in order to do right by (1) the people whose work is published in the magazine, (2) those whose name, face or information appears in the magazine and (3) the readers of the magazine.

Because it is the editor's responsibility to set the ethical standards for the magazine's content, and to apply them consistently, issue by issue, the editor must recognize that the magazine owes something to its subjects as well as to its readers. What it owes, above all else, is fairness. Fairness requires that every fact in every story be as accurate as thorough research can make it. It requires the presentation of opposing views in controversies. It requires opinions to be supported by reasons.

Fairness requires the magazine to be honest with its readers, its sources, its subjects and its contributors. It requires that the magazine scrupulously avoid misleading, misstating or misrepresenting, either in words or in pictures.

Here's how fairness ethics might be applied in some specific situations.

Photos That Lie

Photographs—actual, retouched or computer manipulated—that purport to portray actual people, places or situations must indeed show them, or the reader must clearly understand that the subjects of the photographs are not the actual people, places or situations. An article on teen-age prostitution that is to be illustrated with photos, for example, should not offer shots of a high school building with randomly gathered students standing outside it—as if the students in the photo are involved in prostitution. If the photo tends to mislead, don't use it. Especially don't use faked photos—staged scenes or situations that purport to be the real thing. Be wary of too-good shots, particularly when they come from photographers you don't know well. There's a chance they might have been staged. Choose photographers you trust. Let them know you want only honest shots.

Reconstructed Quotes

Ever since the 1960s, the rise in popularity, among writers, editors and readers alike, of the so-called new journalism has moved many magazines not only to permit the reconstruction of dialogue but to demand it of writers. And so a conversation between individuals is reconstructed, based on the report of one or more sources, and presented to readers as the actual conversation, just as if the dialogue had been tape-recorded. Editors are not unanimous in their views of such reconstruction. Some don't see the need for it. Others question its legitimacy. Probably most, however, would either expect it, believing it enhances a piece's readability, or would at least allow it, seeing nothing wrong with it.

The argument to be made for reconstructing dialogue, besides the fact that it enhances readability, is that virtually all quotes from primary sources—the people who said them or heard them said—are reconstructed. They are reconstructed by the sources. No person equipped with merely a normal memory can hear or take part in a conversation, particularly a lengthy one, and later recall, word for word, exactly what was said. The best that writers are going to get from the sources is their recollection of the actual words spoken. And so to insist on verbatim quotes is to limit the story to paraphrase, except for the conversation's pithiest, most memorable parts—the equivalent of sound bites on television and radio.

Writers and editors should have more freedom than that. They should be given liberty to reconstruct dialogue *based on the recollection of the sources.* Here again the object is fairness; the question to be asked by the editor is, "Does this reconstruction of dialogue treat the participants in the conversation (or alleged conversation) fairly?"

In most cases, reconstructed dialogue contains nothing controversial or potentially litigious. When it does, the editor must proceed with caution, remembering not only the principle of fairness but the laws of libel and privacy.

Fabricated Quotes

They're different from reconstructed quotes. Reconstructed quotes come from the writer's sources. Fabricated quotes are made up by the writer. They are fiction. They don't have a place in journalism. In journalism, what purports to be true must be true—or true to the best of the sources' knowledge or memory. Fabricated quotes are neither.

Cleaned-Up Quotes

Is it permissible, many young writers and editors want to know, to clean up a source's language? To straighten out his grammar and syntax so he doesn't seem a gross ignoramus? To remove obscenities, blasphemies and other offensive words and expressions? To delete "uhs" and "wells" and say-nothing words and repetitions?

The answer: It depends.

The first thing for the editor to remember is that the magazine is not obliged to make a source or subject look good, to dress him up a bit by making him sound literate, reasonable or coherent. The principle of fairness, in fact, may require that the source or subject be shown to the reader accurately, with the same observable defects that the reader would have noticed had the reader, instead of the writer, met and talked with him—especially if those defects help characterize the source or subject. A profile, for example, should attempt to capture the subject in words, and what the subject says, as well as the way he says it, helps capture him for the reader, for good or for ill. When bad or objectionable language (including opprobrious remarks) is part of the person, it is appropriately left in the piece.

In other cases, where the bad language makes no relevant point, where the portrayal of character or personality is unnecessary (the account of an eyewitness to the subject's boat accident, for example), cleaning up the language may help by clarifying and speeding up the quote. The inclusion of incorrect grammar or objectionable words in such cases makes little sense and has little justification, if any.

Then there are times when the policy of the magazine or the requirements of good taste demand that objectionable words and expressions be excised. In those cases, the best solution may be to paraphrase the source's quotes, avoiding the offending language.

Pickup Quotes and Anecdotes

These are quotes and anecdotes that come not from an interviewed source but from a book or a piece published in another publication. Using them is an acceptable practice *if* the writer clears them with their source, to make sure the author of the previously published piece had the facts straight and quotes right. Pickup anecdotes should be rewritten or, if quoted verbatim, should be credited to the original author and publication.

Pseudonyms

There should be a good and understandable (to the reader) reason for using one, and readers must be told it's a pseudonym.

Ghosting

It's a marriage of convenience, bringing together the person who has a story to tell or something to say and the person who can tell or say it well. Does ghosting, by giving a byline to someone who didn't actually write the piece, deceive the reader? Perhaps, but it's a practice honored by time and it's a publishing fact of life, particularly in magazines and books. People who have words placed in their mouths by a ghostwriter, however, should get ample opportunity to see the words—either in manuscript form or in proofs—and have a chance to change them, if necessary, before they're published under their names.

Approval from Sources or Subjects

Occasionally a subject or a source who will be quoted in a piece will ask—in some cases demand—to see the piece before it is published. Should you let him or her see it and, in effect, censor it?

If the source, whether merely a source or the subject as well as a source, agreed to be interviewed and gave no warning about certain remarks being off the record, either just before or just after he said them, the piece may include anything the source said and the editor and writer are under no obligation to get approval before running the piece. The source can't take his words back or change them to make his quote or himself sound better to the reader. What he said, he said. If it makes him appear foolish, bigoted, insulting, arrogant or whatever, that's tough. He shouldn't have said it in the first place, and certainly not to someone he knew was a reporter who was interviewing him for a piece to be published.

On the other hand, if the editor or writer *wants* the source to see the piece, or part of it, to make sure the quote or technical detail is correct, then show it to him and get his corrections, if there are any.

If a source, as a condition to granting an interview, asks that the piece be submitted to him or her prior to publication, the writer should immediately notify the editor before promising anything to the source. The editor then has to decide how important the source is to the story; if the source is vital and the editor wants the story, there's nothing to do but accede to the source's demand. The editor can decide later, after seeing the source's changes on the manuscript, whether she wants to make them.

One writer tried to arrange an interview with a woman whose young daughter had been swept into a storm sewer and had miraculously survived nearly 24 hours in a huge drain pipe nine feet underground. The woman would not agree to the interview unless her lawyer agreed also, and her lawyer wouldn't agree unless the writer agreed to provide him with a transcript of the taped interview before the article was published. The writer wanted the story and so he promised the lawyer a transcript. He sent the lawyer a copy of the story as well as the transcript. The lawyer had no objection to either, and the story—a pretty good one— ran as written.

The guiding principle: If showing the piece to the source (or the source's representative) is to the magazine's advantage, do it. If it's not, don't do it.

Freebies and Favors

If the sales representative of the company that prints the magazine gives you a weather radio for Christmas, should you accept it?

If the developer of a new vacation resort invites you and your spouse to spend a weekend at the resort, entirely at the resort's expense, should you accept?

If the rental agent of the building where the magazine has its editorial offices offers you a couple of tickets to the home team's game with the Toronto Maple Leafs, should you take them?

If the athletic director of a major university offers you a couple of passes to the university president's sky box to enjoy, with an assortment of VIPs, dinner and a comfortable view of the University of Miami game, should you leap at the opportunity?

To gain a clear perspective on any of those situations, you can ask yourself, "If I weren't the magazine's editor, would I still be offered those freebies and favors?" If the only honest answer is "no" or "probably not," you will quickly realize that you're being courted and not just because of your personality or good looks.

When you're the editor, a lot of people will want to give you things, do things for you, be friendly to you. Almost invariably, when they give something *to* you, they want something *from* you. And you have to decide whether what they want is going to affect the content of the magazine and thus perhaps its readers. You have to decide whether accepting the gift constitutes a conflict of interest: your interest in the freebie versus the integrity of the magazine and of its editor.

Inexpensive Christmas gifts and other small favors from the magazine's vendors or landlord don't present much of a conflict. They may be no more than a way to say "thank you" and they're being handed out to all the other customers or tenants.

Freebies that are more costly, that are more likely to influence the editor's judgment or preferences, and whose givers are more interested in the magazine's content than its business affairs, present a much greater ethical danger to the editor, whose power does not ordinarily extend beyond the editorial content.

The editor should be the reader's representative, not the advertiser's, not the flack's, not the special interest's nor the special pleader's. The editor must resist attempts, by forces both good and evil, to buy him, influence him, neuter him, silence him or otherwise affect his independence of judgment or his loyalty and duty to the magazine's readers.

And ethics aside, for very practical reasons the editor should be careful never to do anything that might compromise him or her in the eyes of the magazine's staff or the magazine's publisher.

So when the bait is offered, no matter how desirable, swim on by.

Index

CPSIA information can be obtained
at www.ICGtesting.com
Printed in the USA
BVOW11s0650270816

460208BV00008B/24/P